JUST Happy to be HERE

Words to encourage, enlighten, entertain

Just

Happy

to be

HERE

Words to...
encourage,
enlighten,
entertain

JUST
Happy
to be
HERE

Words to
encourage,
enlighten,
entertain

To Beth!
Hope you enjoy.
Glenn Dromgoole

Glenn Dromgoole

Cover Photo: The author and daughter Jennifer share a laugh after he was honored as Abilene's Outstanding Citizen of the Year in 2013.

Photo by Thomas Metthe, Abilene Reporter-News

Just Happy to Be Here
© 2022, Glenn Dromgoole

ISBN: 978-0-9973706-9-0

Designed by Tinyah Hawkins/Goofidity Designs

Printed in the USA

Published by TexasStarTrading.com

Just Happy to Be Here is available from online booksellers.
For autographed copies, go to TexasStarTrading.com
or visit Texas Star in downtown Abilene.

Texas Star Trading Company
174 Cypress Street / Abilene, Texas 79601
info@TexasStarTrading.com / (325) 672-9696
www.TexasStarTrading.com

Author Glenn Dromgoole is available for speaking engagements.
Call Texas Star for more information.

A FEW RANDOM TESTIMONIALS
FOR
Just Happy to Be Here

- "Of all the books you could read, this is one of them."

- "I loved the book, but I kind of got lost. Was there a plot?"

- "I couldn't pronounce the author's name, but I liked the book."

- "Most of the pieces in this book are short. So am I. Thanks."

- "I took this book with me to the doctor's office. By the time I finished it, I only had to wait another hour and a half until I saw the doctor."

- "I kept this book on my bedside table. It put me to sleep every night for a month. Thank you."

- "I especially liked the section on 20 Sermons in 20 Minutes, but don't tell my preacher. Oh, yeah, he's also my husband."

- "Some of the stories are kind of serious, some are kind of funny, some are kind of weird. Kind of like my own life."

- "I plan to give this book to all my friends. Then I'll make new friends."

To Jennifer & Denny

—

Lauren & Adam

—

Russ & Rita

—

And always, Carol.

—

You make me happy to be here.

— CONTENTS —

Glenn –

Writer.

Thinker.

Poet.

Storyteller.

Editor.

Friend.

Partner.

Husband.

Father.

Grandfather.

Hymn-singer.

Comma-tologist.

Wordler.

Thank you for being you.

-Carol Dromgoole

I hope that something in these pages will:

Encourage you.

Challenge you.

Lift your spirit.

Brighten your day.

Bring you joy.

Give you a laugh.

Make you a little happier to be here.

-Glenn Dromgoole

Inspiration and Whimsy

What I have tried to do throughout the book is put together a mix of pieces that might be encouraging and others that might elicit a smile or a chuckle. If there's an overriding theme here, it is this: Life is to be taken seriously, for sure, but not too seriously. Like you, I'm just happy to be here!

This first section kind of sets the tone, I hope, starting off with three serious but very short articles, followed by a not-so-serious list of favorite hymns that might fit a variety of occupations. Feel free to sing along if the spirit moves you.

A few thoughts related to civility are followed by a couple of upbeat pieces about the importance of good teachers and a softer touch about how grandchildren enrich our days.

In all the sections that follow, I've tried to keep that kind of flow from serious to light, light to serious, back and forth, as it is with our lives. I hope you enjoy the ride and maybe find a few passages you want to share or even read aloud.

The One-Minute Graduation Speech

I have never been asked to give a commencement address and probably will never be invited, but I have given it some thought. What would I tell the graduates? What wisdom would I try to leave them with? Here are my thoughts, condensed into about one minute.

Graduates, families, and everyone else:

First off, I want to follow the two rules of graduation speeches. The first rule is: Keep It Short. The second rule is: Keep It Short.

So here's what I have to say — in one sentence, seventeen words — describing what I consider a good working philosophy for life. A mission statement, perhaps. At least something worth striving for.

It is this:

Wherever I am, I can do something to make my corner of the world a better place.

Wherever I am, I can do *something* to make *my corner of the world* a better place.

I hope that wherever you go, whatever you do, whatever situation you find yourself in, you will try to make your corner of the world a better place. Be kind. Be generous. Be compassionate. Be honest. Be reasonable. Be thankful. Make a difference with your life.

And then I would sit down.

We're Not Computers

Computers can do amazing things. They have incredible memories. They can store millions of facts, figures, and names in their "brain."

But, you know, a computer can't appreciate the beauty of a sunset.

It can't know the joy of hearing a newborn baby's first sound.

It can't experience the excitement of catching a fish or hitting a home run.

It can't take pride in watching a child walk across the stage and receive a diploma.

As great as its capacity for memory might be, it can't remember a mother's love or a grandmother's hug or a wife's caress.

It can't know a father's courage or a brother's character or a sister's loyalty.

It can't measure the depth of a friendship.

A computer may be a smart machine, but it can't be as wise as a good teacher.

It can't hope for a better tomorrow.

It can't believe in anything.

It can't know pain or failure or disappointment, but neither can it know elation or satisfaction or contentment or happiness.

A computer can't feel. It can't care. It can't be generous.

We can, and that's the difference.

What's Your Net Worth?

I stared at the question on the form. It asked simply: What is your net worth?

Well, I had never stopped to figure it. What's my net worth? Not much, I imagine. Maybe, if I'm lucky, it comes out a little above zero.

But as I gave the question more thought, I realized I couldn't possibly answer it. Could you?

Net worth is measured in dollars, but real worth can't be counted that way.

How much is a loving husband or wife/companion/best friend worth?

How about your children or grandchildren? How much are they worth? (On a good day.)

Aren't your memories worth something?

What would you give for the experiences you've had?

Who can put a price tag on friendships?

How much would you take for your freedom?

I had the kindest mother anyone could ever have. How much has that been worth over the years?

Laughter is free but invaluable. What's the net worth of a sense of humor?

Principles certainly count for something. But how can they be measured in dollars?

What would you take for your self-respect, your conscience,

your integrity? Are they for sale?

The value of an education is much greater than its cost. But how much?

Life itself is the ultimate treasure. Can you place a value on it?

Most of what is important in our lives cannot be bought or sold. It has *value*, to be sure, but not *monetary* value. It can't be measured; it can't be counted. But it is what makes life truly rich.

We're all a lot richer than we think, aren't we, when we stop and add up our true net worth.

They're Singing Our Song!

You may have seen a few of these lines before on the internet or in church bulletins, but to my knowledge no one has gone in as much depth – if you call it that – on the subject as I have here, matching church hymns with people's occupations or stations in life.

I must admit that on a few occasions I have let my mind wander from the pastor's sermon as I turned the pages in the hymnal, chuckling at some new additions to my list. I don't recommend it. But I suggest it's better than sleeping. At least you won't snore.

Golfer's hymn: *Swing Low*

Baker's hymn: *When the Roll Is Called Up Yonder*

Psychologist's hymn: *Come, Ye Disconsolate*

Optometrist's hymn: *Turn Your Eyes Upon Jesus*

Optician's hymn: *Be Thou My Vision*

Ophthalmologist's hymn: *Open My Eyes That I May See*

Weight Watcher's hymn: *There's a Wideness in God's Mercy*

Weather forecaster's hymn: *There Shall Be Showers of Blessing*

Weather forecaster's revised hymn: *The Unclouded Day*

Painter's hymn: *How Great Thou Art*

Mathematician's hymn: *Count Your Blessings*

Electrician's hymn: *Send the Light*

Complainer's hymn: *Lift High the Cross*

Complaint desk attendant's hymn: *Must Jesus Bear the Cross Alone?*

Shoeshine attendant's hymn: *Shine, Jesus, Shine*

Produce manager's hymn: *Rescue the Perishing*

Realtor's hymn: *Ivory Palaces*

Fisherman's hymn: *Shall We Gather at the River?*

Flood insurer's hymn: *Higher Ground*

Baseball batter's hymn: *Seek Ye First*

Baseball base runner's hymn: *Lord, I'm Coming Home*

Roofer's hymn: *We Are Climbing Jacob's Ladder*

Emergency medical technician's hymn: *Revive Us Again*

Sandblaster's hymn: *The Solid Rock*

Men's clothing salesman's hymn: *Blest Be the Tie*

Geographer's hymn: *In Christ There Is No East or West*

Restaurateur's hymn: *Let Us Break Bread Together*

Juror's hymn: *I Know Whom I Have Believed*

Judge's hymn: *Tell It to Jesus*

Lawyer's hymn: *Only Trust Him*

Politician's hymn: *Standing on the Promises*

Confectioner's hymn: *Sweet, Sweet Spirit*

Doctor's hymn: *The Great Physician*

Nurse's hymn: *Nothing But the Blood*

Hematologist's hymn: *There Is Power in the Blood*

Proctologist's hymn: *Guide Me, O Thou Great Jehovah*

Asthmatic's hymn: *I'll Praise My Maker While I've Breath*

Dentist's hymn: *Crown Him with Many Crowns*

Census taker's hymn: *All People That on Earth Do Dwell*

Dry cleaner's hymn: *O for a Faith That Will Not Shrink*

Gossiper's hymn: *O for a Thousand Tongues*

Philanthropist's hymn: *The Church's One Foundation*

Shopper's hymn: *A Charge to Keep I Have*

TV station manager's hymn: *I Need Thee Every Hour*

Banker's hymn: *Jesus Saves*

Policeman's hymn: *Yield Not to Temptation*

Thief's hymn: *Steal Away*

Detective's hymn: *Were You There?*

Crime scene investigator's hymn: *There Is a Fountain Filled with Blood*

Debater's hymn: *Almost Persuaded*

Boss's hymn: *Give of Your Best to the Master*

Hotel manager's hymn: *Abide with Me*

Birdwatcher's hymn: *His Eye Is on the Sparrow*

Telemarketer's hymn: *Jesus Is Calling*

Bodybuilder's hymn: *All Hail the Power*

Lottery winner's hymn: *O Happy Day That Fixed My Choice*

Ballet dancer's hymn: *Amazing Grace*

Football coach's hymn: *Pass It On*

Football recruiter's hymn: *Glorious Things of Thee Are Spoken*

Pilot's hymn: *I'll Fly Away*

Receptionist's hymn: *Why Do You Wait?*

IRS hymn: *Is Your All on the Altar?*

Plumber's hymn: *Who Is He in Yonder Stall?*

Young mother's hymn: *Never Alone*

Librarian's hymn: *Let All Mortal Flesh Keep Silence*

Band director's hymn: *We're Marching to Zion*

Tennis player's hymn: *Serve the Lord with Gladness*

Carpenter's hymn: *The Nail-Scarred Hand*

Procrastinator's hymn: *One Day*

Repairman's hymn: *Morning Has Broken*

Songwriter's hymn: *There's within My Heart a Melody*

Travel agent's hymn: *I'll Go Where You Want Me to Go*

Dog walker's hymn: *He Leadeth Me*

Researcher's hymn: *Ask Ye What Great Thing I Know?*

Geometry teacher's hymn: *Will the Circle Be Unbroken?*

Highway patrolman's hymn: *Pass Me Not*

Tracker's hymn: *Footprints of Jesus*

Groupie's hymn: *I Stand Amazed in the Presence*

Sound engineer's hymn: *Angels We Have Heard on High*

Energy auditor's hymn: *Let the Lower Lights Be Burning*

Elementary principal's hymn: *What Child Is This?*

Skier's hymn: *Whiter Than Snow*

Archeologist's hymn: *Rock of Ages*

Concrete contractor's hymn: *How Firm a Foundation*

Sunbather's hymn: *Heavenly Sunlight*

Funeral director's hymn: *Man of Sorrows*

Genealogist's hymn: *O God, Our Help in Ages Past*

Canoer's hymn: *Like a River Glorious*

Accountant's hymn: *The Old Account Was Settled Long Ago*

History student's hymn: *There's Something About That Name*

Lifeguard's hymn: *Throw Out the Lifeline*

Commuter's hymn: *Where Cross the Crowded Ways of Life*

This Hymn's for Them

The preacher gave a thought-provoking sermon on the problem of alcohol abuse and the disease of alcoholism – even among churchgoers.

He cited figures indicating that of every one thousand people who attend church on any given Sunday, seventy might be alcoholics.

Of the two hundred in attendance that day, not counting children, that would mean maybe fourteen alcoholics in the room. About one in every other row.

Maybe the person in front of you, or behind you, or even next to you.

As we pondered those possibilities, we stood to sing the closing hymn:

"Breathe on Me."

The Wondrous Cross

My father had been diagnosed with Alzheimer's and we were taking a trip down memory lane, heading to San Antonio to visit the city where he had grown up and started his career as a minister.

The cassette was playing a selection of hymns featuring the London Philharmonic Choir and the National Philharmonic Orchestra, and we were singing along.

As we pulled into Fredericksburg, "When I Survey the Wondrous Cross," my dad's favorite hymn, came on and we sang heartily – his clear tenor blending with my bass. It was a special moment that we shared.

All that week we shared special moments together. We laughed together and we wept together. Mostly we celebrated together. We celebrated his life, and our lives, and the promise of life everlasting.

Four and a half years later the congregation celebrated my dad's life at his funeral. We celebrated the joy, the faith, the optimism, the commitment, the courage, the hope, the love that we felt his life had represented to us. And, of course, we sang "When I Survey the Wondrous Cross."

I think of my dad every time I hear that great old hymn by Isaac Watts. It doesn't make me sad; rather, it lifts me up, especially the words in the fourth stanza: "Were the whole realm of nature mine, that were a present far too small; love so amazing, so divine, demands my soul, my life, my all."

It was as if Isaac Watts had my father in mind, way back in 1707 when he penned those words, for indeed the love represented by that wondrous cross would become his soul, his life, his all.

And so it has for millions of Christians for more than two thousand years. The cross, that vile instrument of infamy and death, was transformed into a symbol of hope and love and grace that would change lives, indeed would change the world.

It would inspire people like Isaac Watts and the legion of saints before and since to follow the teachings of the Prince of Peace, the Resurrected Savior, the Light of the World, to devote their lives to service, to try to make their corner of the world a little better place.

As Jesus hung there suffering and dying, Scripture tells us, even then in his agony on the cross, he turned to the habitual criminal hanging next to him and granted him redemption and mercy. The horrendous cross, for that dying criminal, became the wondrous cross. It became personal.

Today we hang crosses on our walls, wear crosses around our necks, bow before crosses in our churches. We "Lift High the Cross," we cherish "The Old Rugged Cross," we sing about the "Amazing Grace" represented by the cross.

And perhaps today, or tomorrow, or one day, we come to realize that the wondrous cross is more than a song, more than a symbol, more than an object of inspiration.

We come to realize that it is personal and life-changing, or can be.

When that happens, maybe we can join with Isaac Watts in singing from deep in our own soul, "When I survey the wondrous cross, on which the Prince of glory died, my richest gain I count but loss, and pour contempt on all my pride."

Is There a Place Where We Can Meet?

One of us thinks abortion is simply murder, period. One of us thinks the government shouldn't be able to tell a woman what to do with her body.

One of us says the government should not have the power to require anyone to be vaccinated. One of us says universal vaccinations are reasonable safeguards for public health.

One of us believes President Trump did more than any president this generation to restore pride in being an American. One of us believes President Trump did more than any president in history to destroy democracy.

One of us agrees with what we hear from Tucker Carlson. One of us agrees with what we hear from Stephen Colbert.

One of us posts right-wing diatribes on Facebook. One of us posts left-wing rants on Facebook.

One of us quotes the Bible to support our political point of view. One of us quotes Jesus to contradict that point of view.

One of us says history should be taught the way it always has been. One of us says history should be more inclusive of other points of view.

One of us wants to ban books we consider inflammatory. One of us sees that as dangerous to free expression.

One of us sees a Communist in every Democrat. One of us sees a Nazi in every Republican.

One of us believes our point of view is just common sense

and anything else is nuts. One of us believes our point of view is reasonable and anything else is irrational.

And, yet. Both of us are proud to be Americans. Both of us would rather live here than anywhere else. Both of us may be friends, or church members, or business associates, or relatives.

Is there a place where we can meet? Is there a way we can say - I might be right, you might be right - I might be wrong, you might be wrong - but can we talk? And, somehow, find a way to get along with each other, even if we don't agree.

If we can't find that middle ground, some common table at which to sit, what does it mean for our future as a nation, as friends, as colleagues, as families?

We are different people with differing thoughts. We are not enemies.

Civility Champions

The world needs more Civility Champions in our communities, our homes, our workplaces, our politics, our churches.

People who treat everyone with a little more respect.

- Who try to find some common ground with those with whom they disagree.
- Who consider the possibility at any given time that "I could be wrong."
- Who look for an opportunity to make a small difference for good every day.
- Who go out of their way to praise exceptional service.
- Who teach their children to say "please" and "thank you."
- Who practice the "please" and "thank you" rule themselves.
- Who make their home a place of acceptance and openness.
- Who display good manners as a way of respecting others.
- Who embrace good sportsmanship and encourage their children to.
- Who advocate for reason.
- Who walk through life with a thankful spirit.
- Who count their blessings, then count them again.
- Who reject the ravings of those with simplistic solutions to complex problems.

- Who practice their religion rather than argue it.
- Who are easy to get along with.
- Who believe in the future and work to make it better.
- Who slow down and take time to be more courteous.
- Who take the high road.

Civility Champions make their corner of the world a better place.

A Long-Stemmed Rose

We don't have to do great things to make a difference. Each of us is capable of performing little acts of kindness in whatever we do.

A woman told me this story.

It was Super Bowl Sunday. The woman, a grandmother of seven, was grocery shopping. She had made her way to the checkout line. Three or four other shoppers with full baskets were ahead of her, and there was a little space between them and her.

A young man – she figures he must have been 17 or 18 – suddenly cut in the opening in front of her. When he realized what he had done, he apologized and started to move to the rear of the line.

"Since he had only a long-stemmed rose and I had a full basket of groceries," she said, "at my insistence he remained in line.

"We talked about the Super Bowl game. I commented that he must have someone very special to buy her a long-stemmed rose. He assured me that he did."

When the young man got to the checkout counter, he told the checker to charge him for two roses and he would go get another one. Then he turned and handed the woman behind him the rose and thanked her for letting him break in line.

"I was speechless," she said. "I thanked him and assured

him he had made my day, as I was feeling low and alone on that Sunday."

She didn't get the young man's name, but she never forgot his thoughtfulness.

"I hope he received as much pleasure in giving as I did in receiving the beautiful red rose."

Try Giving Yourself Away

My all-time favorite book is *Try Giving Yourself Away* by David Dunn, the pen name for Robert Updegraff. I have twelve copies of it as I write this, and I've given away quite a few others over the years. I even made it the theme for our church's stewardship campaign one year.

The book first came out in 1947 and has been reprinted several times. The anecdotes in the book may be a bit dated, but the message – the concept – is as valid today as it was when it was written.

One of the editions offers this summary of the book on its cover: "A cheerful, heartening book which sets forth a hundred simple things that you can do to make your life much happier...And to make the world around you a better place to live... Starting right away!"

Updegraff/Dunn was a businessman who made it his hobby to find little ways to brighten someone else's day.

"I took up giving-away as a hobby," he said, "because I found that it made my life more exciting and broadened my circle of friends. I became a happier person.

"Nobody ever found real and lasting happiness in being completely selfish – not in the whole long history of the world. It seems to be a law of life that we enrich ourselves most when we *give* ourselves most fully and freely."

Here are a few of the things he learned to give away:

- A phone call to an old acquaintance he hadn't talked to in several years.
- A compliment to the chef for a good meal.
- A note to an author of a magazine article or book he enjoyed.
- An idea to a business for a slogan or an advertisement, with no strings attached.
- Finding opportunities to give credit to others.

He said there are so many things we have to give: Our time, our experience, our abilities, our influence, our understanding, our tolerance, our good will, our courage, our faith, our sense of humor, our optimism, our smiles.

Giving is not just about money. Giving is about how we decide to approach life.

"This book genuinely changed how I live," an on-line reviewer wrote just a few years ago. "It gave me a different view on what it means to think about other people, and how you can give gifts and the effects it can have."

"I read it," wrote another reviewer, "then I lived it. I still do."

The author said giving-away is "the finest heart tonic in the world" because it not only lifts one's spirit but also stimulates circulation and "makes you feel alive and full of health."

As far as I know, *Try Giving Yourself Away* is out of print now. But you can find it on most used book web sites. I look for it at the used book sale that our Friends of the Library put on every summer. I consider it a successful sale if I can find a copy of that book, and most of the time I do.

And then I take great pleasure in giving the book away and telling the person I am giving it to why it is my favorite book.

"The secret of successfully giving yourself away," wrote David Dunn, "is not so much in calculated actions as in cultivating friendly, warm-hearted impulses. You have to train yourself to obey giving impulses on the instant – before they get a chance to cool. When you give impulsively, something happens inside of you that makes you glow, sometimes for hours."

I came across a quote from Fred Rogers (*The World According to Mister Rogers*) that fits in with what David Dunn/Updegraff wrote about. "The real issue in life," he said, "is not how many blessings we have, but what we do with our blessings. Some people have many blessings and hoard them. Some have few and give everything away."

What Great Teachers Do

They make us care.

They light our fires.

They plant a seed.

They walk the talk.

They have the passion.

They offer hope.

They try harder.

They hang on.

They take pride.

They write in the margins.

They maintain their cool.

They rock the boat.

They laugh often.

They connect the dots.

They stay in touch.

They know they count.

They find satisfaction.

They grow in grace.

They touch our minds.

They touch our hearts.

They touch our souls.

They believe in themselves.

They believe in us.

They keep the faith.

They start early.

They keep going.

They don't give up.

They build bridges.

They spread the word.

They find a way.

They take action.

They wait patiently.

They show up.

They blaze new trails.

They have a heart.

They seize the day.

They keep trying.

They love summer.

They take a break.

They challenge us.

They explain again.

They turn on the lights.

They share ideas.

They want to know.

They cheer us up.

They encourage thought.

They find the moment.

They impact lives.

They set standards.

They take an interest.

They go beyond.

They inspire us.

They make us think.

They ask us why.

They work hard.

They reap rewards.

They cherish victories.

They cut through the fog.

They open doors.

They open eyes.

They push themselves.

They stay young.

They really matter.

They see the big picture.

They take a chance.

They look for pearls.

They see potential.

They trust their instincts.

They plug away.

They make a difference.

They live forever.

They change the world.

Teachers Two by Two

A FABLE IN TRIBUTE TO A NOBLE PROFESSION

God said to Noah as he prepared to embark,
"How many teachers do you have on the ark?"

Noah looked at his list: "We have two surveyors,
two lawyers, two doctors, and two aging soothsayers.

"Two dentists, two writers, two artists, two preachers,
two builders, two sellers…but apparently no teachers."

"No teachers?" said God, "then how do you plan
to pass along knowledge while we look for dry land?

"This isn't a cruise, Noah, it's not a vacation,
it's more important than ever to learn multiplication.

"And biology and music and literature and fitness -
and woodworking, too, as you are my witness."

"But, God," said Noah, "good teachers are rare,
and you expect me to find a compatible *pair*?

"We're shoving off tomorrow or as soon as we can,
there's not time to prepare a complete lesson plan.

"I still have zebras and cheetahs to get on the boat,
and we're missing one fox and an angora goat."

So God said to Noah, "Here's what I will do,
I'll look over my files for a teacher or two.

"You go on with the business of filling the ship,
I'll find you some teachers to take on the trip.

"I know where to look, or at least where to start,
When you need a good teacher, look first in the heart."

The clouds were building and it was starting to rain,
the passengers on board had begun to complain.

It was humid and crowded and dirty and stinking,
the lawyers were suing, the writers were drinking.

The ark was now filled with all kinds of creatures,
except for two wise and exceptional teachers.

Then a man and a woman appeared on the scene,
they seemed sure of themselves, very calm and serene.

They stepped on the boat and drew lots of strange looks
as they began to distribute outlines and workbooks.

"We're teachers," they said, "not saviors or sages,
your assignment for tomorrow is the first thirty pages."

What Grandchildren Do

They make us laugh.
They love our cooking.
They hold our hands.

They listen to our stories.
They laugh at our jokes.
They give us hope.

They make us proud.
They keep us young.
They come to visit.

They go back home.
They like our songs.
They draw us pictures.

They show us their
 favorite things.
They enjoy our company.
They squeal with delight.

They learn from us.
They teach us.
They lift our spirits.

They take us for walks.
They like to wear hats.
They tell silly jokes.

They play in the tub.
They romp in the snow.
They splash in puddles.

They tell us their age.
They blow out the candles.
They whisper their secrets.

They like us as we are.
They seek our counsel.
They renew our faith.

They know how to have fun.
They like to play games.
They want to read books.

They smile for the camera.
They cheer us up.
They enjoy eating ice cream.

They feed our dreams.
They keep us on our toes.
They go to sleep.

They make funny faces.
They share their toys.
They think we can
   do anything.

They shower us with
   sweet kisses.
They surprise us.
They challenge us.

They give us something
   to talk about.
They bring us great joy.
They comfort us.

They revive our souls.
They ham it up.
They make up games.

They grow up.
They give us special presents.
They awaken our senses.

They show off.
They have so much energy.
They wear us out.

They extend the family tree.
They connect the past
   and the future.
They make family
   reunions fun.

They brighten our corner
   of the world.
They give us reason to brag.
They make us happy.

They look forward to
   seeing us.
They never cease to amaze us.
They remind us of what
really matters.

They delight us.
They welcome a new day.
They cry when we leave.

They think we're special.
They touch our hearts.
They know we love them.

A Grandfather by Whatever Name

When my daughter Jennifer was pregnant with her first child, she called one day and said, "Dad, what do you want to be called when the first grandchild is born?"

It was a perceptive question, especially considering what MY grandfathers went by.

One of them was Bot. The other was Dang-Dang.

"If you don't want to be Bot or Dang-Dang," Jennifer said, "you might want to give it some thought."

I don't know why Dang-Dang was called that. The oldest cousin came up with the name, and he used it for both of his grandfathers – Dang-Dang Sharber and Dang-Dang Cox. The rest of us followed suit.

As for Bot, I asked my Aunt Frances one time how Bot became Bot. She wasn't sure, but she figured that my oldest cousin Patsy named him.

As a toddler, Patsy was living with her grandparents, Emmet and Anna, who tended to shout a lot at each other.

"ANNA?" Emmet would holler from three rooms away.

"WHAT?" Anna would answer in an equally loud voice.

And so we had Gana and Bot.

Before Jennifer was born, my mother made it clear that she wasn't going to be Granny, or Gana, or Mammaw, or Mimi. She would be called Grandmother. My dad preferred Paw-Paw. That was settled.

On the other side, my mother-in-law became Mommers. Her husband had died many years earlier, but Jennifer would ask Mommers to tell her about Mr. Mommers. Made sense.

Youngsters, or maybe the grandparents themselves, have come up with some creative monikers over the years.

At grandparents.com you can find dozens of examples for grandmothers, from the most popular to such exotics as Bamboo, Uddermudder, Jammagramma, Gitchey, MaxiMa, PomPom, and Cha-Cha.

Grandfathers include Baboo, DooDad, Doozy, Faux Pa, Jeepers, Paddles, and Splash.

No Dang-Dangs or Bots, however.

And no mention of Gaggie, which is what my grandchildren call me.

It wasn't hard for us to settle on that name. After all, my little brother started calling me Gaggie when he was a toddler, and in my family I've been that ever since.

I figured I might as well stick with it. And I have now, as a grandfather for twenty years - and, I hope, for a few more.

My Dad and I Didn't Play Catch

From the time I was 10 until 16 or 17, I lived and breathed baseball. I played Little League, which was as far as one could go in our little town. We didn't have a high school baseball team.

So I coached Little League in high school. I played church league softball, ironically for the Methodists even though my dad was the Baptist minister. (The Baptists had a full lineup already; the Methodists needed a catcher for their Catholic pitcher.) I took up writing about sports as a way to match my interests with my talents.

On a few occasions growing up my dad took me to a minor league game, and I suppose there were some times when we went out in our spacious front yard and played catch. But I don't remember many such moments.

Dad was a good preacher, but he didn't seem to be much of an athlete, and frankly at that age I was a lot more interested in sports than church.

The few times I do remember my dad pitching the ball to me, I thought that he looked rather awkward. He didn't seem to have a natural throwing rhythm.

Dad would sometimes show up at my games, but he didn't say much and he wasn't one of those fathers who would get out and coach his son and teach him the finer points of the game. Years later, when my dad was in the early stages of Alzheimer's

Disease, we took a trip back to his hometown of San Antonio. He told me stories on that trip I had never heard before.

One of them had to do with baseball.

He told about how he had been such a big baseball fan as a child. He had a catcher's mitt, and he and his brother would spend hours playing catch.

He listened to the San Antonio minor league games on the radio and even dreamed of maybe being a professional baseball player himself someday.

Then one day some of the neighborhood kids started teasing him about how he threw the ball. They said he threw like a girl. He said he was so embarrassed that he never played baseball anymore.

He wept as he related that story. So did I. He went on to say that throughout his life he tried to never make fun of the way a child did something. He said that incident taught him how a comment can break a child's spirit.

My dad and I rarely played catch. Finally, so many years later, I understood why. How I wish now that we could have connected on something we both loved.

The Clothes We Keep

With spring lurking around the corner, it seemed like an appropriate time for a little spring sorting.

We're talking about clothes: Those pants that somehow have shrunk a size or two while hanging in the closet; that colorful Hawaiian shirt that seemed so much fun three or four years ago but hasn't been worn since; that suit that was a hand-me-down ten years back, at least; a pair of lounging pants, or pajamas, with the tag still on them; that cheap T-shirt picked up in Galveston that never did fit all that well after the first washing.

They've been bundled up to give away, with the hope that someone who doesn't have two bulging closets and three drawers full of clothes will find them useful.

But, after that, after casting aside a dozen shirts, eight pair of pants, the aforementioned suit, and more, the closets don't look all that empty, the drawers still barely close.

And it's no wonder why. Some clothes we keep because we need to – a suit or two for church or funerals; enough long-sleeved and short-sleeved shirts, dress and casual, for all seasons; slacks and khakis and jeans and two or three sport coats; plenty of shorts and T-shirts for summer lounging.

If that were all, however, they would fit nicely in one less closet and one less drawer. But some clothes we keep not just because they still fit, but because they have some deeper meaning. The clothes we keep - like the books we keep or the dishes we keep or the boxes of unsorted family pictures we keep or a lot of the other stuff we keep – remind us of something that is, or was, significant in our lives, something we want to hang onto a little while longer and cherish the memories.

Why else would we keep ten, count 'em, Friends of the Library shirts – some from the annual book sale, others from the book festival? Parting with them would be like giving away a favorite book - so they stay. Plus, what would we have to wear when book sale and book festival time rolls around?

What about that hideous pair of madras shorts hardly ever worn? Well, it was a gift from grandchildren who got a huge kick out of giving it and still do on the few occasions the shorts sneak out for an appearance - when they visit.

A well-worn T-shirt from that trip to Niagara Falls? The ragged one from the Texas Book Festival, presented to featured authors several years ago? The funny ones that say things like "Careful, or you'll end up in my novel" or "Hymns: The Original Soul Music" that were delightful gifts from that special someone? Two three-quarter-length T-shirts from a favorite burger joint? The one with a picture of the old high school, long since torn down?

Of course, they stay. They stay because the space they occupy in the closet does not begin to compare to the space they occupy in our mind.

Some clothes we keep because we need to. Others because, well, we need to.

20 Sermons in 20 Minutes

Most sermons are fifteen to twenty minutes long or longer. All week preachers read reverently, study prayerfully, write creatively, hoping their sermons will touch someone's life.

They quote Scripture, tell relevant stories, offer three or more points, maybe throw in a joke or two or a poem or a popular song or a sports illustration. Some speak from a manuscript, some from notes, some from memory - all from the heart.

I appreciate the work, the study, the effort that goes into preparing a good sermon that touches hearts and changes lives.

But what if…

What if the preacher stepped into the pulpit one Sunday, offered his or her thoughts in a few words – an executive summary, just a minute or two - and sat down?

How might we react?

"You call that a sermon?"

"Maybe we ought to start paying him by the word instead of by the week."

"I didn't even have time to take a nap."

"Yay! We got out early."

Well, here are some very short sermons for your

consideration. Hopefully, they all convey a relevant spiritual message. See what you think.

First, A Call to Worship These Days

I was glad when
they said unto me:
"Let us now turn off
our cell phones."

Jesus's Three-Point Sermon

1. Love God.
2. Love each other.
3. Love your enemies.

Do *these things* in remembrance of me.

Amen.

Five Words of Faith

Much of the Christian faith can be characterized, or summarized, in the words of these five old hymns:

- "Jesus loves me, this I know."
- "Amazing grace, how sweet the sound that saved a wretch like me."
- "Count your many blessings."
- "Joy to the world."
- "Brighten the corner where you are."

Love.

Grace.

Gratitude.

Joy.

Service.

Five words of faith to live by.

Amen.

All We Ask

And what does the Lord require of you but to do justice, and to love kindness, and to walk humbly with your God? – Micah 6:8

All we ask:

- A grateful heart
- A kind and loving soul
- A principled courage
- A quiet generosity
- A joyful sparkle
- A humble spirit

Amen.

A One-Word Sermon

Today's sermon is only one word: BYKOTA.

When I was growing up in church, BYKOTA was the name of the older women's Sunday school class.

They may well have been the biggest gossips in the church. They knew what was going on, and they were inclined to whisper it among themselves. You didn't cross the BYKOTAs. They had their choice of Sunday school rooms.

And, yet, when someone in the church was sick, or there was a death in the family, the BYKOTA Class was the first one there with a comforting casserole, or two, or three.

BYKOTA. What does that word mean?

It's from Paul's letter to the Ephesians, chapter four, verse thirty-two: Be Ye Kind, One to Another.

B Y K O T A.

Be Ye Kind, One to Another.

Be Ye Kind, One to Another.

Make that a six-word sermon.

Amen.

A Psalm by Any Other Name

Scripture: Psalm 24

Hello. We Psalms have to stick together. Particularly those of us who aren't all that famous.

Take my brother. He's not just Psalm 23 – he's The Twenty-Third Psalm.

Everybody knows him. Preachers quote him at funerals. People write whole books about him. Children and dogs follow him everywhere.

"Why can't you be like your brother, No. 23?"

"Because I'm No. 24," I say. "I'm my own person, I mean, Psalm."

I may not be the most quoted, the most revered Psalm in the Bible, but I'm in there. Psalm 24 - or as I like to call myself, The Twenty-Fourth Psalm.

I do have a pretty good line in verse ten when I say, "The Lord of hosts, he is the King of glory."

Well, I like it. Especially at Christmas when great choirs sing, "Glo-oh-oh-oh-oh-oh Oh-oh-oh-oh-oh Oh-oh-oh-oh-oh-ria."

You don't have to be the greatest Psalm to have worth. God loves me for who I am and for what I can do, and he doesn't expect me to be someone else.

He made me The Twenty-Fourth Psalm, and that's good enough for me.

Amen.

Jesus Laughed

Jesus laughed! That is the text of today's sermon.

Now you may be thinking, I don't recall that verse in the King James Bible. I remember "Jesus wept" but not "Jesus laughed."

But read your Bible again, and you may find examples of where Jesus surely must have laughed.

Remember the story about how a rich man's chances of getting into heaven were roughly equivalent to a camel squeezing through the eye of a needle? That was hyperbole. Jesus laughed. At least we hope he did!

He took a pitcher of well water and turned it into the best wine anybody had ever enjoyed. Bet that was a fun wedding reception.

He's preaching to five thousand people, and all of a sudden it's dinner time, and nobody thought this Jesus guy was going to preach so long, so nobody brought food. Except this one kid. He had heard preachers before, and he knew how they could get wound up, so he packed his lunch box.

So Jesus says to his sidekicks, "Hey, you guys get everybody to sit down, and bring me the kid's lunch box, and we're going to feed all five thousand people."

"Hey, Jesus, that's a good one. Ha-ha-ha-ha-ha."

Well, you know the story. Everybody had plenty to eat, and they even had to ask for doggy bags.

Then there was the time Jesus walked on water and scared the wits out of his disciples. Surely he got a little chuckle out of that.

Laughter is a gift from God. It is a gift we can share to brighten our own lives and those around us. Of course, there are times when we can't laugh or shouldn't laugh. But aren't there more times when we *could* enjoy life but choose not to? Find the joy. Rejoice in it.

Amen.

Why Go to Church?

Why do we go to church?

To praise and worship God?

To see friends?

Because it's a habit, it's the right thing to do?

To be inspired by a sermon?

To sing hymns or hear good music?

All of the above?

I think I would say, simply, I go to church to recharge my spiritual batteries.

The call to worship one week put it this way:

"As persons who never fully live up to their high calling in Jesus Christ, we come to be encouraged to do our best for one more week."

To be encouraged to do our best for one more week. Or as the preacher put it in his sermon that same week, "Jesus says, 'Follow me and do as I do.'"

I certainly need to be encouraged to do that.

Amen.

What We Believe

I grew up in a church that said it didn't believe in creeds, so we didn't recite the Apostle's Creed or any other formal creed.

Yet, there were those in the church who turned right around and demanded that all of us subscribe to one kind of creed or another – that we believed the Bible to be literally true, word for word handed down by God Himself; or that we believed that abortion was wrong in all circumstances; or that we believed that only our church had a lock on the Truth; or that if you were a Christian, you had to vote a certain way.

I think Christians, over the years, have talked too much and argued too much about what we believe and have spent too much time and energy trying to convince each other that we're right and the other folks are wrong.

Let me tell you what I believe.

I believe we shouldn't worry so much about trying to prove that we're right.

I believe we shouldn't try to bottle up God and put our own label on Him.

I believe we should go about doing good and being kind to people.

I think that's what it means to be a Christian. That's what it means to be the church.

Amen.

You Are the Church!

*For this sermon, the preacher walks out from behind the
pulpit. He smiles. He asks the congregation to stand.*

You are the church.

The sermon is not what I preach. It is what you live.

The preacher is not the church.

The choir is not the church.

The organist is not the church.

This building is not the church.

You are the church.

Preach your sermon every day.

Amen.

Think a Billboard Thought

For billboards to be effective, they need to have a simple message stated in a few words.

What is your billboard thought? If you could proclaim your message to the world in seven words or less, what would you say? It's a good way to evaluate your own priorities as well as your outlook on life.

What is your message? Is your billboard positive or cynical? Does it raise others up or put them down?

The philosopher Aldous Huxley said that after spending his entire lifetime pondering the human condition, the most profound thought he could pass on could be summarized in six words.

His billboard thought: "Try to be a little kinder."

I expressed my own billboard thought as the title of one of my books: "More Civility, Please."

Jesus's billboard thought: "Love God. Love your neighbor."

St. Paul's billboard thought: "And the greatest of these is love."

What's yours?

Amen.

Thanks for Showing Up

In her later years, my friend Betty Moor was so hard of hearing that she couldn't hear thunder. But every Sunday and Wednesday you could find her at church.

Someone asked her, "Betty, if you can't hear the sermon and you can't hear the music, why do you keep coming every week?"

Betty's eyes twinkled and she smiled.

"Well, I want everyone to know whose side I'm on."

Sometimes it takes a lot of effort just to show up, to be there week after week, to smile, to be supportive, whether at church or at community events or family gatherings.

But, think of this, if no one made the effort to show up, there wouldn't be church, there wouldn't be concerts, there wouldn't be family get-togethers. Or at least they wouldn't be the same.

That was certainly brought home during the Covid pandemic, when so many events had to be cancelled because we *couldn't* show up. We Zoomed instead, and while that was better than nothing, it wasn't quite the same thing as being there.

It was reassuring when we could show up again. It reminded us that we do have that power – the power to make our presence felt.

The multitude of saints who have gone on before us surely

include those super faithful, like Betty Moor, who found a way, week after week, to show up, to be there, to smile and say, "I want everyone to know whose side I'm on."

Amen.

Gifts We Take for Granted

The Gift of Life – full of possibilities.

The Gift of Time – ours to use wisely.

The Gift of Laughter – the language of joy.

The Gift of Talent – little things we do well.

The Gift of Work – making a difference.

The Gift of Generosity – giving what we can.

The Gift of Kindness – in word and deed.

The Gift of Praise – opening our hearts.

The Gift of Peace – with ourselves and others.

The Gift of Forgiveness – given or received.

The Gift of Sacrifice – unselfishness in action.

The Gift of Gratitude – a thankful spirit.

The Gift of Faith – something to believe in.

The Gift of Hope – anticipating the future.

The Gift of Love – the greatest of them all.

Amen.

You Just Won the Lottery

When you think about it, in many ways we've already won the biggest lottery of them all – the lottery of life.

We won the lottery when we received the gift of life and health.

We won the lottery when we were born into a free country and a good home.

We won the lottery when we received an education that allowed us to read and think and earn a good living.

We won the lottery when we were given so many blessings we often take for granted – plenty to eat, a comfortable home, a little money in the bank.

We won the lottery when we learned about a loving God who promises to be with us forever.

Millions of people around the world, people in this country, and right here in our community would be delighted to trade places with us – for we are truly lottery winners.

Lord, help me live my life in perpetual gratitude and find ways to express that gratitude by being more understanding, more accepting, more generous, more loving

Amen.

The Hamburger Sermon

We all love hamburgers, but we don't all love them the same way. I like mine with cheese, with mayo (but not too much mayo), with lettuce, tomato, pickle, onion, on a toasted bun. One meat patty, not two. On a charcoal grill, preferably.

My wife takes hers without cheese, just lettuce and meat patty only. Maybe a little barbecue sauce.

How about you? How do you like yours? I read that there are more than a million different ways to have a hamburger. One million.

We're all different, not just in hamburgers but in so many, many other more important ways. There are not a million ways – there are billions of ways – in which we are different.

And God loves all of us just the way we are. He loves each of us as he loves all of us. He loves you. He loves me. He loves us all.

Mayo or mustard or, yes, even ketchup. With or without onions. Meat-based or plant-based. Fast food or steakhouse or home grilled. Republican or Democrat or Independent. Black or White or Brown. Rich or poor or in between.

God says, "Have it your way. Do it your way. I love you."

Amen.

In the Spirit

A spiritual life,
it's been shown
throughout time,
doesn't require tomes
of a doctrinal plan.
It's simply trying
in all things
to be kind,
and doing for others
whatever we can.
Amen.

A Sermon About Patience

Dear God,
Please grant us the gift of patience.
Right now!
Amen.

Manna from Heaven

God sent down manna from heaven (Exodus 16) to feed the grouchy, quarreling, starving Israelites. So what was manna, anyway, or maybe the question is what it wasn't.

We can be assured of ten things that it wasn't:

10. ICE CREAM. It would melt before the Israelites could agree on a flavor.

9. PIZZA. The Romans weren't all that highly regarded in biblical days.

8. HAMBURGERS. Cut the pickles, hold the onions, mayonnaise or mustard?, cheese?, double meat? Too many potential disagreements.

7. FRIED CHICKEN. Not on the approved subsistence diet for wilderness people.

6. FRENCH FRIES. Who are the French? We're talking Israelites here.

5. DONUTS. Although that does sound a lot like manna.

4. SHRIMP. Not in the middle of the desert.

3. BARBECUE. Where's the sauce?

2. ENCHILIDAS. Beef, cheese, or chicken, with or without rice and beans?

1. MESQUITE GRILLED STEAK. Something that heavenly surely would have merited its own scripture verse.

Today, we are blessed with unlimited manna.

A gift from God? Everything is a gift from God.

Do we, unlike the Israelites, remember to say thanks?

Amen.

The Agnostic's Sermon

What if a noted agnostic — not an atheist, but an agnostic, a doubter, a skeptic - was invited to give the sermon one Sunday? Of course, that's not likely to happen. But what if... And what if he (or she) got right to the point?

> Oh God
> (If there is a God)
> Save our souls
> (If we have souls).

An Attitude of Gratitude

A Thanksgiving sermon

An Attitude of Gratitude is an approach to life that makes life itself more enjoyable – for us and everyone we touch.

An Attitude of Gratitude is:

- Being helpful rather than critical.
- Seeing the possibilities rather than the objections.
- Seeking out the joy in life and embracing it.
- Accepting the imperfections in others the way we hope they accept ours.
- Finding time for a smile, a warm thank you, a phone call, a note, a touch, a hug, a handshake.
- Believing there is so much to be positive about.
- Understanding that life is to be enjoyed, celebrated, lived, shared, loved, given.
- Feeling good about ourselves and about others.
- Appreciating the things we have rather than taking them for granted.
- Hoping for the best and expecting it, from ourselves, from others, from the future.
- Reaching out with a helping hand because we were helped when we were helpless.

An Attitude of Gratitude could change our lives if we gave it a chance. It could change our world.

Amen.

Stable Gifts for Today

And, finally, a short Christmas sermon

Please join us at the stable, where we have come searching for meaning on this special day.

After the presents are opened, and the songs sung, and the dinner enjoyed, we look around to find the lasting gifts of today are not under the tree, but are here, in a simple and familiar stable:

- The *love* of a parent.
- The *life* of an infant.
- The *promise* of an angel.
- The *faith* of a shepherd.
- The *generosity* of a wise man.
- The *guidance* of a star.
- The *peace* and *joy* and *hope* of a Christmas.

May these gifts be yours today and throughout the year.
Amen.

Language Matters

I was the first born to an educated couple. My mom had been elected county school superintendent at age 27, and my dad was an aspiring young preacher. Good grammar was expected from their son.

When I was 3 or 4, the story goes, I was outside playing with the boys from across the street when one of them said, "I ain't got no" (whatever he didn't have).

"Don't say 'I ain't got no,'" I chided him. "That's a double negative."

"A whaaaat?" he replied.

Of course, I don't remember this. But my folks told the story often enough, so it must be true.

Language matters. Grammar matters. Words matter. That's what this section is about, but it's not all serious. Some of these pieces play with words, have fun with words. And punctuation, too.

The section starts off with more cliches than you can shake a stick at, comments on a few grammatical obsessions, deals facetiously with misplaced commas, and ends with way too many puns in "I Could Have Been a Masseuse… But I Rubbed People the Wrong Way."

Food for Thought Is Sign of the Times

As an award-winning author, I figured there was no way under the sun I could, in good conscience, include more than a hundred common clichés in a single article in a highly respected publication. Read 'em as you weep.

In the best of all possible worlds, writers should avoid cliches like the plague. But beggars can't be choosers.

With all due respect, a bird in the hand is worth two in the bush. Between you and me and the gatepost, a writer had better be safe than sorry. Our actions speak louder than words.

On the other hand, it goes without saying that, for better or worse, sometimes we can't see the forest for the trees, and the left hand doesn't know what the right hand is doing. Then we have to let the chips fall where they may since we can't have our cake and eat it, too.

In other words, we have to fish or cut bait. One has to have both feet firmly planted on the ground to see the handwriting on the wall and proclaim, "Do as I say, not as I do."

That's the way the cookie crumbles, I suppose. We have to take the bitter with the sweet and overcome a lot of adversity. It's an uphill battle because the grass is always greener on the other side of the fence.

Not to beat a dead horse, but sometimes we bite off more than we can chew. We find that we can't be all things to all people, and we have to go back to the drawing board and try to make heads or tails out of it.

If worse comes to worst, we can always take it like a man and hope we come up smelling like a rose.

But that's putting the cart before the horse. In the long run, if we burn the candle at both ends, seize the bull by the horns, call a spade a spade, and dot the i's and cross the t's, there is not a ghost of a chance that our stories will be as dull as dishwater.

Remember, the early bird catches the worm.

However, if we get up on the wrong side of the bed and become satisfied that half a loaf is better than none, we are in danger of jumping out of the frying pan into the fire and turning out copy that isn't worth a hill of beans.

Instead, we need to go whole hog and fall head over heels in love with the Mother Tongue. My English teacher would turn over in her grave, if she had bitten the dust, at the way good writing is dead as a doornail these days.

It's enough to drive a teacher up the wall. It certainly isn't a case of the blind leading the blind. They sweat blood, but when all is said and done, you can lead a horse to water but you can't make him drink. You can't make a silk purse out of a sow's ear, and you can't judge a book by its cover.

By the same token, you can't teach an old dog new tricks, and that comes straight from the horse's mouth. It's six of one, half-dozen of another.

What really rubs me the wrong way – and let's not beat around the bush about it – is the way some writers become too big for their britches and add insult to injury at the drop of a hat by an easy-come, easy-go attitude.

Well, I wasn't born yesterday. The bigger they come, the harder they fall. That's the way the ball bounces.

How do you like them apples?

There's an unwritten rule for most writers that it's either feast or famine. We're all in the same boat. Either an article is an albatross around the neck, or we can write until the cows come home. Sometimes we can't squeeze blood from a turnip, and other times when it rains, it pours.

At times like that we don't look a gift horse in the mouth or cut off our nose to spite our face because some day we know the chickens will come home to roost and we'll be barking up the wrong tree.

We'll just have to cross that bridge when we come to it, if we don't burn our bridges behind us.

That's a horse of a different color, and I wouldn't touch it with a ten-foot pole.

The bottom line in writing is, don't count your chickens before they're hatched. It's a dog-eat-dog world out there, and we have to turn over a new leaf and play our cards right if we expect to hit the nail on the head through thick and thin.

It's a whole new ball game these days, and we need a shot in the arm if we expect to come full circle and pull ourselves up by our bootstraps between the devil and the deep blue sea.

Speaking of the devil, you took the words right out of my mouth.

Reading the Obits

I've reached the age where the obituaries are the first thing I tend to read when I pick up the local newspaper or call it up online.

I joke that I average the age of the obits to see what it might say about my own mortality. If the average age on a given day is higher than mine, then I figure I might have a little more time left. However, if the average age is lower than mine, it might be cause for concern. Not that I have a lot of control over it, one way or the other.

On this given day, seven of the sixteen people listed in death notices in the local paper were older than me; nine were younger. Uh-oh.

Seriously, though, I read the obits to stay informed on who died that I might know, or a relative I might know. On this day, for example, the father of one friend was in the obits, and the mother of another friend.

I like it when obits reflect something of the personality of the deceased. Some obituaries just list dates and lists of survivors, but the best-written ones offer a flavor of the person's priorities and, sometimes even, their peculiarities.

"He managed to attend eight colleges in four years," one obituary noted, "playing football at most, before graduating from Hardin-Simmons with a degree in geology – and through an administrative kindness excusing his scant chapel attendance."

Another one: "His mama spanked him every morning when he woke up just to get it out of the way for the day."

Things like that really make the person "come alive," so to speak.

When I wrote my mother-in-law Ellen's obituary in 2019, I tried to incorporate some of the qualities and quirks that made her life special.

"Ellen created quilts for her grandchildren and great-grandchildren and enjoyed shelling black-eyed peas, cream peas, and pecans and making plum jelly, peanut brittle, fruit cake cookies, and pickles for family members and friends. Her turkey and dressing, corn casserole, peach cobbler, and pecan pie were the highlight of family holiday dinners - and her fried chicken was legendary.

"Ellen's weekly hair appointments approached the level of religious fervor, as did the viewing of favorite TV shows, especially 'Dancing with the Stars,' 'Wheel of Fortune,' 'Jeopardy,' 'Downton Abbey,' and the Little League World Series. She spent a minor fortune on magazine subscriptions in her eternally hopeful but ultimately futile quest to win the Publishers Clearinghouse Sweepstakes."

Years ago, at the *Fort Worth Star-Telegram*, the editor told staffers to write their obituaries and put them in a file in case something happened to them. Evidently, a reporter had died suddenly, and no one knew enough to put together a good obit.

George Dolan, the paper's humor columnist, filed his obit. One sentence read: "I regarded Dolan as a son," mused editor John Ellis, "of a bitch." Another line requested that the directors of the Star-Telegram Credit Union serve as pallbearers. "They carried me when I was alive. They may as well finish the job."

A Legacy

I have to admit I really do care
what they say at my funeral
even though I have a good excuse
for not being there myself.

Whole Books in Six Words

Writer friend Caleb Pirtle challenged readers of his blog to write stories in just six words. He cited a classic by Hemingway: "Baby shoes. For sale. Never worn."

Caleb offered a few of his own: "Fast cars. Fast women. Funeral tomorrow." "She left. I'm alone. Whiskey sour."

It got me to thinking about six-word stories, or even books, in various genres.

History

The Alamo. Lost battle. Won war.

Travel

Drove all day. Still in Texas.

Sports

Friday night. Winning touchdown. New girlfriend.

Memoir

Blue pond. Skinny dipping. Clothes gone.

Business

Oil boom. Made fortune. Blew it.

Biography

Born. Drank. Found Jesus. Quit. Died.

Motivational

Summer roofing. Got message. Studied harder.

Theological

Jesus loves me. This I know.

Mystery

Boyfriend cheated. Poisoned him. Became nun.

Western

Bad guys. Stolen horses. Hanging tree.

Romance

Can't stand each other. Become lovers.

Children's

Once upon a time. The end.

Cookbook

Pretty pictures. Difficult recipes. Dine out.

Academic

Introduction. Text with footnotes. Conclusion. Index.

Just Yesterday

When I worked at the *Fort Worth Star-Telegram*, we had two distinctly different newspapers – the *Morning Star-Telegram* and the *Evening Star-Telegram*. We had different staffs, different editors. We competed against each other.

We also had different styles when it came to how we referred to time. For example, the *Evening Star-Telegram* could use the words yesterday, today, and tomorrow in stories because the articles were being published the same day they were written.

But the *Morning Star-Telegram* frowned on those words. They preferred to use the day of the week – Monday, Tuesday, etc. If a writer said something was happening "today," for example, the reader might be confused as to whether that meant Monday, when the story was written, or Tuesday, when the story was read.

The *Morning* staff copy editors were quite diligent in making sure that yesterday, today, and tomorrow were edited out and replaced with the proper day of the week.

And so, one day, a reporter was quoting a person who insisted that he was not naive about something that was going on. "I wasn't born yesterday," he contended.

Of course, that raised the automatic red flag on the *Morning* edition copy desk.

And the next day, so the story goes, the newspaper quoted the man saying: "I wasn't born Tuesday."

You're Welcome

We were having dinner at a restaurant. The waitress was very good. When our glasses were half-empty (or, I suppose you could say, half-full!), she was there to refill them.

"Thank you," I said.

"You're welcome," she said.

It wouldn't have been appropriate, but I wanted to stand up right there and hug her!

She said, "You're welcome." Not, "No problem."

And because of that, she received a bigger tip than I would usually leave.

Most of the time when we're having lunch or dinner somewhere and we receive good service from a waiter or waitress and we thank them for their attention, their response will be, "No problem."

No problem? Of course, it's no problem. We're not a problem, we're the customer, for goodness' sakes. Without us, you wouldn't have a job, so don't tell us that it's no problem to give us good service!

Their tip just went down.

One day a friend took me to lunch, and he brought up the subject about how "no problem" had somehow replaced "you're welcome." We agreed that we liked to hear "you're welcome" after we had said "thank you."

He paid for lunch. As we left the restaurant, I said, "Thank you for lunch."

And he said with a straight face, "No problem."

I don't think he was trying to be funny. The irony of the moment never dawned on him.

Thank you. You're welcome.

Thank you.

You're welcome.

Between You and Me

The story is told about a veteran copy editor at a newspaper who kept a note in his pocket which he consulted often.

A young editor watched the older man take the note out of his pocket, unfold it, look at it, fold it up, put it back in his pocket.

After observing this exercise several times, the young editor took the older editor aside and asked him: "I just have to know about that note you keep in your pocket. It must be something profound. You look at it several times a day. Will you share it with me?"

"Sure," the old editor replied. He took the note out of his pocket, unfolded it, looked at it, and handed it to the young editor. The note read: "i before e except after c."

Well, I wish some people would carry a note in their pocket about the use of the pronouns "I and me." Specifically, "between you and me," "to my wife and me," "for him and me."

In the cosmic scheme of things, I suppose it doesn't really matter all that much whether we say "to he and I" instead of "to him and me." But how has this petty ungrammatical irritant taken hold and spread – like a plague of pestering fire ants – across the linguistic landscape? Have we become a nation of grammatical illiterates?

"She is going to take Melba and I to lunch."

"It has been a privilege for he and I to be associated with

the program."

"It is important to we businessmen."

"It's so funny to watch he and John."

"That's of particular interest to my wife and I."

"This is just between you and I."

These statements came from the mouths of educated people – university presidents, preachers, professors, newspaper publishers, business leaders, etc.

I've been ranting about this for at least forty years, several times in print, and I'm about to wave the white flag and surrender. No, I refuse to do that. I'll just grimace, silently curse, maybe stifle a groan.

How do you correct a friend or a colleague or a fellow board member or any other adult without coming across as the fuddiest of duddies? I once asked facetiously, in print, that if readers had any suggestions on how to handle this, "please send they to I."

It is really quite simple. How would the pronoun sound if used by itself? You wouldn't say "She is going to take I to lunch." "It has been a privilege for I to be associated with the program." "It is important to we." "It's so funny to watch he." "That's of particular interest to I."

Of course, that doesn't work for "between you and I." Maybe, like the old editor, it takes a note: "between you and me." Consult it often, especially when speaking in public or on television.

The Grammar Police

Even though I would like to,
I don't go around correcting
people's grammatical mistakes,

like when someone says,
"She met with Jane and I" –
or "Me and John went to town."

I cringe, I want to scream,
with Jane and *me*! Jane and *me*!
John an*d I* went to town."

You wouldn't say, "She met with I"
but rather "She met with me" -
so it should be "with Jane and me."

And "Me and John" as subjects of a sentence
violates every rule your English teacher
tried to teach before simply giving up.

I favor a five-dollar fine for "with Jane and I,"
maybe ten – or more - for "Me and John"
as the subjects of a sentence.

But instead I just suffer in silence
because who wants to be around
the grammar police anyway?

If there were a grammar Crimestoppers,
a lucrative reward for anonymous tips -
I'd turn them in and collect my fee.

It Matters, Where You, Put Those, Commas

Commas are, important and shouldn't just be, thrown in, anywhere. Like some, people, apparently do.

With some, writers it's like they, have a bucket full of commas and they, feel compelled to, use them all, somewhere. So they just, take their manuscript or their, memo or letter, and their, bucket of commas and, give the bucket, a good shake and willy-nilly pour it, out and *voila*, they have, commas, everywhere whether they make any, sense, or, not.

I have, actually read, books where, that seems to be the, case. They have, a seemingly unlimited supply, of commas and they're going, to find a way, to use all of, them. A good, editor, might have trimmed the number, of excess, commas but apparently a good, editor, hadn't been, available.

Commas should, be used judiciously in, my, opinion. More, periods and less, commas I say. But not, everyone, shares this, view.

And it's not, just books but also, letters and, memos and e-mails etc. Even, conversation. You may have heard, the example given of how a comma, can dramatically change the meaning, of a sentence: "Let's eat grandma." Or "Let's eat, grandma."

A simple rule of thumb is to put a comma where a pause is needed. No pause, no comma.

But that, rule, doesn't seem to be applied, all that often,

anymore.

There was a new bank, in town last year that promoted, itself as "Making Abilene, Happy." After a, while, the bank dropped the, offensive comma - which, did make some folks in town, happy.

We were praying a printed, confession in, church the other day and to, my horror, there was a comma, error right there as we were, trying to be, contrite and, confessional.

I, refuse to confess to a comma, error and I said, so, to my wife which, wasn't probably the most, appropriate time to, get into that because, it almost made her, laugh, out, loud which, would have spoiled, the mood, of being repentant for the, whole, congregation.

Still I, have to think that even though, God created, commas He intended us, to use them the way our, English teachers, tried to teach, us. But evidently we, weren't paying too, much attention, to what the teacher, was saying because we, were more interested, in how the football, team or the basketball, team or the band, was doing or what our friends, were wearing and didn't really care, about the significant, but more limited role that commas, should play in our writing. All those red circles, the teacher, put around our wildly misplaced, commas were just to add some, color, to our otherwise, drab D-minus-minus, essays we figured.

So if you, have a bucket full, of commas sitting on, your desk or in, your computer my advice is to do, everyone especially your English teacher a favor, and delete, them. Most of the, commas in this piece could be, deleted.

In short: Fewer commas. More periods. Shorter sentences.

And don't; even get me; started; on semicolons.

Thank, you.

*If you found this piece almost impossible to read, well, that's
the point.*

Commas, in Verse, for Better or Worse

Commas, commas, in my sleep,
Commas, commas, wide and deep,
Commas, commas, I must keep,

Though they make my editor weep.

Commas, commas, left and right,
Commas, commas, day and night,
Commas, commas, I am smitten,

Commas, commas, overwritten.

Commas, commas, so sublime,
Commas, commas, in their prime,
Commas, commas, not a crime,

Commas, commas, all the time.

Commas have a special place,
Commas take up little space,
Commas help me set the pace,

My editor is a basket case.

Any Semicolons Around Here?

It's not often that one gets involved in a good philosophical discussion about semicolons. I happened to observe one. It was what is known in education as "the teachable moment."

Several members of our adult literacy council were visiting a literacy class. The teacher, Judy Berry, was working with six adults who are learning to read and write.

She had the students take turns reading sentences from a beginning textbook. Most of the sentences were short and simple. She urged them to plow ahead through the book so they could get on to more difficult and interesting material.

Then one of the students asked a question. He pointed to something in the textbook and asked Mrs. Berry what it was.

"That's a semicolon," she replied. What happened next was pure art – the art of teaching.

She asked if anyone knew what a semicolon was. No one did. She walked to the chalkboard and wrote a sentence: "I am looking for her; I have money for her." She told the students that a semicolon is used to join two very short sentences.

"What else might we have used to join these sentences?" she asked. "We might have said, 'I am looking for her because I have money for her.' Or 'I am looking for her, and I have money for her.'"

The students joined in the discussion. One said she had never seen a semicolon in the letters she receives. Another thought maybe she had seen one in a letter from school sent home to parents. That sent Mrs. Berry back to the chalkboard to write a sentence that might be sent home from school: "We were going to have a meeting; however, it was canceled."

Another student, probably in his early fifties, said he didn't remember ever seeing a semicolon anywhere in his whole life; maybe they didn't have those when he was in school as a child. Mrs. Berry laughed and assured him that semicolons had been around a long time.

She told the class that the newspaper editor was there and said we probably use a lot of semicolons in the paper. I replied that I "almost never" use them. The teacher looked over a weekly newspaper written especially for beginning readers. No semicolons there.

The discussion had extended beyond the time for class to be over, so Mrs. Berry brought it to an end. But I'll bet those six students were on the lookout for semicolons the rest of the week.

By the way, I came back to the office and searched our Tuesday front page for semicolons. None of the four staff-written stories contained semicolons, but I found seven in two articles from the Associated Press. Of the seven, just one was used to join two sentences (or independent clauses); the others were used to separate items in a series.

But that's another lesson for another teachable moment.

I Am a Period.

I am a period.
I have a myriad
of uses. But the best
is I give readers a rest.
They stop when I do.
My gift to you.

The comma,
on the other hand,
it can't stand
for people to pause,
considers it his cause
to make sentences long,
which I, as a period,
think is quite wrong,
no time to take a breath,
which is the death
of clear writing
and good reading,
so I am pleading,
for the comma to stop,
and maybe swap
that little curly-cue
for a dot or two.

I am a period.
A simple dot.
Use me a lot.
I am your friend.
The end.

Aha!

Most of our days,
most of our years,
most of our lives
are punctuated
with periods, commas,
colons, semicolons,
and question marks.

But when we look back,
we cherish those
special moments
when the only
appropriate response
was, without question,
an exclamation point!

I Could Have Been a Masseuse…
But I Rubbed People the Wrong Way

I could have been a dermatologist… but I got the itch to do something else.

I could have been a butcher… but I couldn't hack it.

I could have been a welder… but I flared up at my boss.

I could have been an astronomer… but I wanted to be a star.

I could have been a soldier… but I quit one March.

I could have had goat farms in several states… but the kids got tired of moving.

I could have run a deli… but I quit cold turkey.

I could have run a tobacco shop… but I wasn't up to snuff.

I could have been a speech pathologist… but I kept hearing strange voices.

I could have been a salesman up north… but I hated making cold calls.

I could have been a nasal spray tester… but I paid through the nose.

I could have been a waiter… but I resented taking orders.

I could have been a lawyer… but I lost the will.

I could have been a switchboard operator… but I had too many hang-ups.

I could have owned a bakery… but I ran short on dough.

I could have been a painter… but I kicked the bucket.

I could have been an accountant... but it was too taxing.

I could have been a ghost story writer... but I couldn't eek out a living.

I could have owned a clock business... but I had too much time on my hands.

I could have been a college president... but I lost my faculties.

I could have manufactured wigwams and teepees... but it was two tents.

I could have been a soap salesman... but I lost the Zest.

I could have been a mattress tester... but I kept jumping from one job to another.

I could have been a potter... but I didn't urn enough.

I could have run a hotdog stand... but I couldn't cut the mustard.

I could have had a tire repair service... but I went flat broke.

I could have been a wine taster... but the spirits didn't move me.

I could have operated a dairy... but I milked it for all it was worth.

I could have been a poker-playing plumber... but I lost everything when I bet on a straight flush.

I could have been a roofer... but I got tarred of it.

I could have been a stand-up comedian at a breakfast diner... but the yolk was always on me.

I could have been a driver for a new fleet of taxis... but I had too much of a Checkered past.

I could have been a famous diet consultant... but I got too big for my britches..

I could have made beautiful combs... but I couldn't part with them.

I could have been a locksmith... but I couldn't find the key to happiness.

I could have had a career with the Corps of Engineers... but I wasn't worth a dam.

I could have been a judge... but I decided to try something else.

I could have been a biology teacher... but there were too many skeletons in my closet.

I could have been a ventriloquist... but all my colleagues were dummies.

I could have raised ducks... but it wasn't all it was quacked up to be.

My Texas

I was born in Texas and have lived in Texas all but one of my seventy-eight years. I was a reporter and editor at the *Fort Worth Star-Telegram* in the '60s and '70s before serving as the editor of dailies in Bryan-College Station and Abilene, even enjoying a year as president of the Texas editors organization.

For nearly eighteen years I helped organize and chair the West Texas Book Festival and wrote a weekly column for several newspapers on Texas books and authors. Since 2004 my wife Carol and I have owned and operated Texas Star Trading Company, a book, gift, and gourmet shop in downtown Abilene that we not-so-humbly tout as the National Store of Texas.

My friend Carlton Stowers and I compiled and published a list of *101 Essential Texas Books* in 2015, and I am the author or co-author of several other Texas books, including *100 Great Things About Texas, A Small Town in Texas,* and *West Texas Stories.*

I may not be the consummate authority on Texas life and culture, but I have over the years observed and written about the Lone Star State on a fairly regular basis. The articles, poems, reflections, and impressions in this section grow out of my love for, fascination with, and enjoyment of our state's character and characters.

You Must Be a Texan If....

You stand up and put your hand over your heart when the band plays "The Yellow Rose of Texas."

You order chicken-fried steak at a fancy French restaurant.

You leave a message on someone's voice mail and tell them, "Give me a holler when you can."

You check the Dallas Cowboys (or favorite college) football schedule before setting your wedding date.

You think "Don't Mess with Texas" was one of the original Ten Commandments.

You talk a cop out of giving you a ticket for an expired car inspection sticker by saying, "I was fixin' to get that done."

Your idea of giving directions includes the phrase "over yonder."

You realize that just because the old Cadillac in front of you has on its right blinker doesn't mean that it won't turn left.

You schedule a vacation to Paris ...... Texas.

You've been stopped for DWY - Driving While Yodelin'.

You wrote your honors thesis in college about Shiner Beer.

You wrote your honors thesis in college while drinking Shiner Beer.

You don't have to be told that Paradise really is in Texas.

You say, "Y'all come back," even if you're speaking to just one person.

You believe Willie Nelson was an Old Testament prophet

in a prior life.

You take your family Christmas pictures in front of the Alamo.

You include your pickup truck in your family Christmas pictures taken in front of the Alamo.

You claim George Strait is your third cousin-in-law.

George Strait really is your third cousin-in-law.

Your ATM password is 1836.

Texas Haiku

A haiku poem makes its point in just 17 syllables — 5 in the first line, 7 in the second, 5 in the third. Here are a few haiku having to do with Texas.

At the Alamo,
offered a prayer to heroes,
bought a souvenir.

In West Texas sky,
stars at night are big and bright,
sing all about it.

Texas getaways:
forests, lakes, beaches, mountains,
wide open spaces.

Texas north to south
runs about eight hundred miles,
also east to west.

Number of counties:
two hundred and fifty-four —
with historic names.

Texas Aggie Band
wins football halftime shows with
precision marching.

Longhorns, Aggies, Bears,
Red Raiders, Mustangs, Cougars –
and, of course, Horned Frogs.

Astros, Cowboys, Spurs,
Rockets, Rangers, Mavericks,
Texans, not Oilers.

If it's Friday night,
whole small town's gone to ball game –
except the sheriff.

Our favorite beer:
Shiner Bock, brewed in Texas –
prior to micro.

Kincaid's in Fort Worth:
best hamburger in Texas
or anywhere else!

So many pickups,
café serves chicken fried steak –
cream gravy, of course.

Mesquite steak dinner
medium rare with two sides –
salad, potato.

Loves Cajun music,
makes pot of gumbo at home –
a Southeast Texan.

Crabs at Galveston,
shrimp, oysters at Crystal Beach –
ferry runs both ways.

Barbecue brisket,
ribs, sausage, beans on the side –
get in line early.

She says, "Howdy, y'all,
'Yont some more catfish, honey?
'Yont iced tea with that?"

Tex-Mex favorites:
enchiladas, tamales,
tacos, nachos, beer.

State Fair concoctions –
ever'thang is chicken fried,
even peach cobbler.

In Texas we say
'Fixin To,' which confuses
people not born here.

We vote in Texas
as early and as often
as they will let us.

Grew up on old hymns –
"When We All Get to Heaven" –
we're already there.

Bride was great with child,
groom quick with a proposal,
father with shotgun.

Tourists come in droves
seeking history and fun –
we take credit cards!

Texas history
not the main reason they're here –
welcome to Six Flags.

Yes, Austin is weird –
people still run for office
so they can live there.

Love being able
to avoid Houston commute –
now office from home.

From Texarkana,
a hard day's drive to Big Bend,
or to South Padre.

Panhandle vista
at Palo Duro Canyon
should be on your list.

Fort Worth rodeo:
cowboys at Cowtown stock show
keep legend alive.

State population
more urban than rural, yet
cowboy culture thrives.

Drive thousands of miles,
enjoy food, fun, history –
never leave the state.

Take your camera
when bluebonnets are in bloom –
almost can't go wrong.

Davy said it best:
You can go to hell, I am
going to Texas.

Texas's Big Wonderful History

Stephen Harrigan has written the best history of Texas — ever.

It's called *Big Wonderful Thing: A History of Texas*, and you want to make sure you don't drop it on your foot. It's almost a thousand pages, however many pounds that might be.

But, the thing is, it's a fun history to read. Wait a minute, did I just use the words *fun* and *history* in the same sentence?

I did, and Harrigan does, all the way through the book. He writes interesting story after story after story, the way a best-selling novelist might write a history book. He focuses on people and anecdotes rather than places and dates and doesn't interrupt the narrative with footnotes. (They're at the back in case you need them.)

Oh, yeah, Stephen Harrigan is better known as a best-selling novelist than as a writer of history books, which may be why *Big Wonderful Thing* is the most comprehensive and most readable book about Texas history.

You pick up a 900-page book that weighs more than you've been trying to lose for the last several years and it's kind of intimidating, like when you were a freshman in college and the professor assigned this "outside reading" that you dreaded opening.

Then you turn to the first page and it's not about Texas history — at least not the way you've always thought about it —

but it's about "Big Tex" at the State Fair and how that is an icon for the Texas we know and love.

And it just gets better and better.

Especially when it comes to the twentieth century, which tends to get short shrift in Texas history books. Harrigan devotes nearly 400 pages – about half the book – to the modern era, beginning with the Spindletop and Sour Lake oil booms and Eastland's Old Rip horned toad to the birthplace or homestead of four U.S. presidents to world wars, civil rights, football, Texas music, and of course the changing Texas political landscape.

Texas history is a lot more than the Alamo, San Jacinto, the Republic years, statehood, and the Civil War, which of course Harrigan covers. Through the years, Texas history has often been white-washed – told from the prevailing Anglo point of view – and Harrigan offers a more balanced perspective without minimizing its heroic nature.

But the bottom line is not the fairness or the inclusiveness of the book, but its readability. It is fun to read. Harrigan knows how to tell a story that makes the reader look forward to the next one.

Big Wonderful Thing took its name from a quote by artist Georgia O'Keeffe, who observed: "I couldn't believe Texas was real ... the same big wonderful thing that oceans and the highest mountains are."

Middle Names

Maybe this can't be proven scientifically, but I suspect that more people in small towns than in large ones, and especially in the South, were called by their first *and* middle names when we were growing up in the '50s.

Among the girls in our town were Mary Ann, Mary Sue, Mary Jane, Mary Frances, Mary Lou, and Mary Alice. Linda Sue, Donna Sue, Bonnie Sue, Carol Sue, Sammie Sue, Billie Sue. Linda Kay, Winnie Kay, Linda Rae, Johnnie Rae.

I knew a Bobby Wayne, Bobby Joe, Joe Bob, Joe Don, Billy Joe, Billy Bob, Billy Glenn, Billy John. James Lee, Ray Lee, Roy Lynn, Roy Lee, and Lee Roy. Joe Neal, Jo Ann, Jo Carrol, Sara Jo. Nita Lou, Linda Lou, Betty Lou. Lou Ann, Betty Ann, Beth Ann, Barbara Ann, Cheryl Ann, Carol Ann. Carol Jean, Barbara Jean, Carol May, Annie Mae, Lettie Mae.

There was Jack Wayne, Carl Wayne, Donald Ray, Martin Ray, John Ray, John Henry. And the Earls - John Earl, Dallas Earl, Robert Earl, Henry Earl, Joe Earl. The Belles and Nells - Lula Belle, Annie Belle, Bertha Belle, Olga Nell, Adria Nell, Birdie Nell. And Frank Stanley, Minnie Lee, Martha Faye, Thelma Lois, and even a Dinkie Ruth.

Maybe I'm just more sensitive to being called by a first and middle name because growing up I was Glenn Allen. My father was Glenn, and after I left home I dropped the Allen and just became Glenn. Which made for some confusion when my dad would come to visit. He became known to my friends as The Real Glenn Dromgoole. Which made me what?

Of course, nearly all of us have middle names. But most don't have to go by them. About the only time most people get called by their first and middle names is when their mother is mad at them: "John Bradenfield Smith, you get in this house right this minute!"

In my hometown and to my family, I am still Glenn Allen even though I've been Glenn everywhere else for sixty years. And so, I'm sure, are Bobby Joe, Linda Sue, Carl Wayne and Mary Alice. Dinkie Ruth, however, long ago dropped the Dinkie.

Vote Dry!

The "wets" and the "drys" have fought in Texas for decades. Texas allows local counties, and even precincts within counties, to determine for themselves whether to allow the sale of beer, wine, and liquor. There are still some counties and a good many precincts that are "dry."

Sour Lake, where I grew up, was "wet" as long as I can remember. But there was one election in the mid-'50s when it looked like Sour Lake might go dry.

All it took to call a wet-dry election was a certain number of signatures, and that wasn't hard to come up with on such a divisive issue. The churches usually could be counted on to gather the requisite number of names on a given Sunday morning.

Of course, just because you signed the petition didn't necessarily mean that you were against booze. Signing a petition was a public declaration, and it was prudent for most small-town folks to be publicly aligned against demon rum. Voting, like drinking, was however a private, not a public, matter.

On this particular campaign, the ministers in town were properly and indignantly aligned against the "wets." More than likely they were quietly encouraged by a would-be bootlegger or two who knew that they could make more money in a dry town than in a wet one.

As the Baptist preacher, my dad was one of the leaders of

the dry forces. Perhaps at that stage of his life he was privately dry as well as publicly, though that would change in time. After I reached adulthood, we would enjoy a little nightcap together, usually accompanied by a pipe or cigar.

But back then, I was ten or eleven and my dad hadn't yet come out of the closet, or the wine cellar. He helped organize a temperance parade through town to urge voters to "Vote Dry!"

It wasn't all that much of a parade, if memory serves, just a few cars and pickups with signs and streamers. Dad was driving a pickup and had several boys my age riding in the back for emotional support.

Suddenly, without consulting my dad, one of the boys started a chant: "Vote Dry! Liquor will gitcha in TROUUUU-ble. Vote Dry! Liquor will gitcha in TROUUUU-ble."

We picked up the chant. All through town we rode, singing at the top of our voices, "Vote Dry! Liquor will gitcha in TROUUUU-ble."

Sour Lake voted wet. Overwhelmingly wet. I don't think the drys ever tried again. I know my dad didn't.

Like Where You Live

I grew up in a small town about fifteen miles from a larger city. When introducing myself, I would say that I was from Sour Lake, and when people said where is that, I would say it is fifteen miles from Beaumont.

During my freshman year in college, however, the upperclassmen told us we should be proud of our hometown and make it the center of our universe. I was taught to revise my introduction to say I was from Sour Lake, and when people asked where was that, I would say that Beaumont is fifteen miles from Sour Lake, instead of the other way around.

Perhaps that's just semantics, but the point was driven home to me that wherever we're from, we should celebrate that. Over the years, as I have lived in just three other cities, I have tried to keep that in mind and look for ways to acknowledge and celebrate the good things about those places.

When I was a young editor in Fort Worth, we published a page of "100 Things We Like About Fort Worth," with contributions from various staffers and readers. Later we published similar articles in Bryan-College Station and in Abilene. It wasn't difficult to come up with a large number of things we liked.

Wherever he traveled, my father-in-law would sing the praises of his hometown – little Albany, Texas. "Have you ever been to Albany?" he would ask a stranger while standing in line. And then he would proceed to tell them something about the town's history. When he died, I wrote a poem about him going to heaven and meeting the Lord and asking him, "Have you been to Albany?" Then he would add, "It might not be heaven, but it's right next door." Certainly that's how he felt about the town where he was born and lived nearly all his life.

Like where you live. Work to make it better. Be a champion for your community.

Somewhere in Texas

If you grew up in a town named Sour Lake, you would have a soft spot in your heart for towns, villages, and wide spots in the road like these:

Buffalo Gap	Ireland	Comfort
Bug Tussle	Italy	Welfare
Coon Creek	Scotland	Ponder
Dog Ridge	Egypt	Necessity
Muleshoe	Tarzan	Poetry
Possum Trot	Honey Island	Blessing
Fairy	Honey Grove	Energy
Fred	Sugar Land	Uncertain
Maypearl	Flat	Utopia
Whon	Pancake	Loving
Old Glory	Bootleg	
Cut and Shoot	Cool	
Gun Barrel City	Wink	
Pointblank	Ding Dong	
Notrees	Dime Box	
Little Hope	Dawn	
Mud City	Sundown	
Africa	Sunset	
China	Pep	
Germany	Happy	

John Erickson: a Texas Literary Hero

I had the good fortune to spend three hours watching a Texas literary hero sign books for his many admirers. It was the most inspirational book signing I've ever witnessed.

John Erickson is the author of the *Hank the Cowdog* series of children's books that were never intended to be children's books. He wrote them for ranch families, but they were discovered by elementary school teachers and librarians – and parents – who found them to be books that especially boys, many of them non-readers, would devour and come back for more.

The stories are told in the voice of Hank, the self-proclaimed head of security at a ranch in the Texas Panhandle, which basically means he barks at everything. Bumbling Hank has a good heart but always seems to find himself in some kind of trouble, usually of his own making. Yet he manages to get through it to bark for another day – even emerging as a hero despite himself. Hank stories are humorous, engaging, uplifting.

During the book signing, whole families – two and three generations – would come up to the table and ask Erickson to pose for pictures after signing their books. This wasn't just any author, they would testify.

I don't know how many times I heard the phrase, "Hank the Cowdog changed my life." Or even, "Hank the Cowdog saved my life."

They would go on to say how they were not interested in

reading as a child, but then they read a Hank novel and were hooked. They became avid readers and better students, went on to college or work, had families, introduced their children to Hank, and their children discovered the joy of reading.

One man said he took Hank tales with him to Iraq during a tour of duty there and spread the word to his fellow soldiers. A woman had a book signed for her 21-year-old son, a former non-reader now a college senior majoring in engineering.

Erickson has heard the testimonials many, many times as he has spoken and signed books at hundreds of schools, libraries, bookstores, and other venues over the years. I'm sure he never tires of hearing them.

The series, which began in the early 1980s with *The Original Adventures of Hank the Cowdog* and *The Further Adventures of Hank the Cowdog*, has expanded to 77 titles, and should easily exceed 80.

Erickson has written a number of other very good books as well, including *Bad Smoke Good Smoke* - about the 2017 Panhandle wildfire that destroyed his ranch home, office, and treasured personal and family possessions. He was inducted into the Texas Literary Hall of Fame in 2019.

But I venture to say that those literary accomplishments pale in comparison to the influence of his *Hank the Cowdog* stories.

At a restaurant after the book signing, the manager spotted Erickson and exclaimed, "My favorite author – Hank the Cowdog!"

What a legacy for a genuine Texas literary hero.

Elmer Kelton: Humble and Gracious

I knew Elmer Kelton, the great Texas novelist, for only about six years. But I became a huge fan and considered him a dear friend.

Elmer won so many awards he hardly had room for them in his spacious home office in San Angelo. Yet, it wasn't the awards that drew people to him and his books. It was his writing, his humility, and his graciousness.

I got to know Elmer in December 2002. I was driving to work one morning at McWhiney Foundation Press at McMurry University, and the thought popped into my head: "I wonder if Elmer Kelton has written a Christmas book."

At the office, I Googled "Elmer Kelton, Christmas" and two stories popped up. I looked them up in the McMurry library, and of course they were excellent stories – one about Christmas at the ranch as a young boy and one about Christmas before going off to fight in World War II.

So, I took the next step. I called Elmer, who didn't know me from Adam. I introduced myself and told him we were interested in publishing a book of his Christmas stories.

"I've only written two Christmas stories," Elmer replied.

"Well, that's all I had been able to find. If you could write one more, I think we could make a small book out of them."

I suggested that the third story might be the Christmas he took his beloved Ann back to her home country of Austria. He had referred to that in another piece.

A few days later he wrote the third story and we had a small book, just 64 pages but with a gorgeous cover painting by H. C. Zachry and a foreword by the Texas poet laureate, Walt McDonald.

Christmas at the Ranch sold well the next Christmas, 2003, and we became friends. Ann smiled and told me it was the first book of Elmer's she had read.

The next year my wife Carol and I opened Texas Star Trading Company. One of the first book signings we had was with Elmer Kelton. We had many more over the years.

One thing we quickly noticed at these book signings was how reverently his readers felt about him.

A common occurrence: An older man and woman would get in line to have a book signed. When they would get to the front, the man would hand Elmer the book to sign and his wife would ask if they could have their picture taken together. The man would stand by Elmer and the wife would snap their picture.

It was like the couple finally had a chance to meet their hero – not a sports star or an astronaut or a politician, but a writer. A writer who touched something in their common experience.

Elmer would stay as long as people wanted him to sign books. We usually scheduled his signings from 1-3 p.m. on Saturdays, but rarely did he finish before 3:30 or 4. One reason his signings ran long was because so many people would want to tell him that his book, *The Time It Never Rained*, must have been written about their father or grandfather.

I heard Elmer say on several occasions that *The Time It Never Rained* was his favorite of all the books he wrote. And it was the favorite of most of his fans as well. I included it in my list of "10 Great Books for Your Texas Library."

The first Saturday of December in 2007 Elmer and Ann were at our store for a book signing. It was a huge day. People not only bought his books but other things in the store as well. By mid-afternoon, it was clear that this would be the biggest sales day in the history of the store, eclipsing the sales record set by the iconoclastic Kinky Friedman, who had run for governor on the ticket, "Why the hell not?"

"Elmer," I said, "you have just set a record for sales in our store, even more than Kinky Friedman. Maybe you ought to consider running for governor."

Elmer immediately deadpanned, "Why the hell not?" and everyone broke up.

Elmer's writing, his wonderful stories, will live on for years to come. But, oh, how we miss his wry wit, his smile, his humility, his character, his great spirit. He was truly one of a kind, a Sandhills boy from West Texas who touched many, many lives.

A footnote: When Elmer died in 2009, he had finished two or three other novels that were published after his death. The first one, Other Men's Horses, he dedicated to me. I felt so honored.

David Davis Wrote Delightful Texas Children's Books

David Davis, one of my favorite Texas children's authors, wrote children's books that adults probably enjoyed and understood more than the children they read them to.

Among his titles: *Texas Mother Goose, Ten Redneck Babies, Redneck Night Before Christmas, Librarian's Night Before Christmas, Texas Zeke and the Longhorn,* and *The Twelve Days of Christmas - in Texas, That Is.*

Here are two of my favorites from *Texas Mother Goose,* which Carlton Stowers and I included in our selection of *101 Essential Texas Books.*

Breakfast with Humpty Dumpty

Humpty Dumpty sat on a wall
Humpty Dumpty had a great fall
All the ranch cowboys and all the vaqueros
Got a big breakfast of huevos rancheros.

Three Blind Mice

Three blind mice,
See how they run!
They ran for Senate up Austin way,
Since they're blind it's the place to stay;
They're just like senators in every way,
Those three blind mice.

David had a wonderful sense of humor and often teamed up with fellow Fort Worth children's author Jan Peck to put on delightful programs for schools, libraries, and book festivals.

One time David and I did a book signing together and were virtually ignored while folks literally lined up out the door to get former Texas Tech football coach Spike Dykes to autograph his new book, *Tales from the Texas Tech Sidelines*.

We joked that never again would we try to compete against a football coach at a book signing.

A Short Personal History of the Telephone

The other night when the phone rang at our home – yes, we still have a landline (I really don't know why) – I picked it up only to hear, once again, "Hi, this is your personal health representative," or maybe, "I'm calling to let you know that…" or simply, "Don't hang up."

Instead of just hanging up, as I usually do, I yelled into the phone, "Well, hello, if this is a real person, I'm so glad to be speaking to you, and if it isn't a real person, then get the heck off my telephone!" Except I didn't say "heck."

Of course, it wasn't a real person. It was a recording, which is about all we ever get on our landline – and now it seems on our cell phone as well.

It got me to thinking back about my personal history with the telephone, going back more than seventy years. Maybe you can relate.

When I was just four years old, growing up in a small town in Texas, the telephone was much more personal. I could pick up the receiver in our house and the operator would come on the line and I would say, "I need to speak to my daddy," and she would say, "Sure, Glenn Allen," and would ring his office.

My grandparents lived in the country, and they were on a party line. Four long rings and you answered the phone. Three long rings and it was Mr. Cox. If you wanted to make a call, you had to make sure no one else was already using the line. (And, of course, you could gently pick up the phone and eavesdrop on other folks' conversations – not that we ever did that!)

Fast forward a few years. I'm a teen-ager and the phone rings and I make a mad dash to answer it before my mother can. But she gets there first and hands it to me with a smile and that enticing possibility, "It's for you!"

Remember collect calls? It's your mom's birthday, and at 11 o'clock at night you remember. You're in college, or in the Army, or just starting a new job, you don't have much money, so you call collect to wish her a happy birthday. And your dad's glad to accept the call because at least you remembered her birthday this year.

There's the call when you tell them there's someone you want them to meet and you're bringing her this weekend. The call when the first child (the first grandchild) is born. The call when a parent has passed away. The call you never even expect to dread - a grown child has died suddenly.

And pay phones. The plane lands and there is a mad rush to the bank of pay phones to check in with the office. You hardly ever see a pay phone these days. The lyrics to a country song make no sense to this generation: "Here's a quarter, call someone who cares."

There's the first cell phone in a bag not much smaller than a suitcase, but you could make calls from your car – is this the new age or what? – if you're within a mile or two of a cell tower.

All of a sudden, people are not just talking on cell phones, they're texting. You don't even have to talk anymore if you can type with your thumbs. You don't have to have a conversation with the people you're having dinner with. You have a phone. They have phones. Just text each other.

When you get home, you can call and see the grandkids on your phone. Way back when, you figured it was some futuristic fantasy that we would actually be able to see each other when we spoke to them on the phone. And now, instead of a collect call, we can call mom or sis or brother and sing happy birthday while looking at them in person.

You call the office and ask your young associate to look up something in the phone book for you. It gets very quiet. "What's a phone book?"

Wow, the telephone is such a remarkable thing! We have been so incredibly fortunate to be personal witness to how it has transformed our lives, has brought families together in their own living rooms though separated by hundreds, even thousands, of miles.

What a gift!

And then the phone rings, and with great anticipation you answer it.

The recorded voice says, "Don't hang up." But you do.

A Favorite Tex-Mex Recipe

Here's a quick, easy, and fairly healthy recipe I use when I'm in the mood for dinner with a Tex-Mex flavor. I'm not a great cook, but I can whip this one up and enjoy it, with enough usually left over for the next day.

Around our house, we call it "Mexican Glenn."

Ingredients
1 lb. lean ground beef
½ small onion, diced
1 t. garlic powder
2 t. taco seasoning
1 cup instant rice, uncooked
1 cup beef broth (or beef bouillon)
Can of corn, drained
Can of pinto beans, drained
Can of black beans, drained
Can of diced tomatoes with green chilies, not drained
Grated cheese
Flour tortillas, tortilla chips, or corn chips
(Optional) Top with salsa, sliced avocado, guacamole

Instructions

1. Cook the ground beef and onion together in a large skillet on medium high heat until beef is no longer pink. Drain grease.

2. Sprinkle the beef with garlic powder and taco seasoning.

3. Mix the rice, broth, corn, beans, and tomatoes in a bowl.

4. Pour mixture over the beef. Stir.

5. Bring mixture to a boil. Cover, reduce heat and simmer for about 20 minutes until rice is tender. Stir occasionally.

6. Top with grated cheese and cook another 2-3 minutes.

7. Serve as a meal by itself, or wrapped in a flour tortilla, or over crispy tortilla or corn chips.

8. (Optional) Top each serving with 1 or 2 T. of salsa, a dollop of guacamole, or sliced avocado.

Note: This dish can be made mild, medium, or hot, depending on the diced tomatoes and salsa you prefer. For more spice, add a few chopped jalapenos. We prefer it mild.

Serves 4 to 6 people. If it's just my wife and me, we'll have enough for two meals and then freeze some.

Texas Weather

Heavy rains are predicted in Beaumont of course,
snow flurries likely at Amarillo and Morse.

Watch out for tornadoes around Wichita Falls,
to beat the heat in Dallas hang out in the malls.

They're fryin' in Bryan, it's clear in the East,
there are blizzards in Winters (until noon at least).

A norther is blowing from Lubbock to Post,
there's a hurricane watch on the Texas Gulf Coast

Drought conditions continue around Abilene,
the Hill Country's having the worst flooding they've seen

After scanning the radar, I think you could say -
for Texas weather it's just a typical day.

Way-uhl, Hay-uhl

We had a weatherman in Texas and, way-uhl,
he didn't quite learn to pronounce hay-uhl.

He just never understood that the word hail
in Texas is a two-syllable word - hay-uhl.

Evidently he had been trained for a spell
in the Midwest and was taught to say hell.

So he would predict that golf-ball-sized hell
was about to hit our area, and when it fell -

We were relieved that it was only hay-ull
and that Satan wasn't staying for a spay-ull.

The weatherman left after a why-uhl
but we still remember him with a smy-uhl.

The Cowboy Spirit: Lessons for Life

I've never been a cowboy, never lived on a ranch, never worked a rodeo or a roundup, never even owned a horse. I have written a country music song or two that never went anywhere. I told my editor all that, but she insisted, since I was a writer and lived in Texas, I could write something about cowboys, and so I did. For more authentic writing about cowboys, read John Erickson, Red Steagall, or Elmer Kelton.

Cowboys - working ranch hands, rodeo daredevils, or cowboy painters, composers, writers - have important things to teach us about life, if we are open to the lessons.

Cowboys know who they are, wherever they are. The cowboy spirit can be embraced and embodied on the ranch or in the city, dressed in faded jeans or a business suit, driving a battered pickup or a new sedan. The true cowboy spirit is found on the inside, deep in the heart, in the substance of the soul.

Cowboys watch and listen. A cowboy will tell you that a good rule for learning is to keep your eyes open and your mouth shut.

Cowboys hang on when the going is tough. A bull rider has to stay on the bull for eight seconds, which can seem like an eternity when you're the one riding. A good rule for us when facing tough times: Try to hang on just a little longer.

When cowboys get bucked off, they get back on. And so must we. When we flunk a test or lose a big sale or make a mistake that costs our team or company dearly, like the cowboy we have to get back in there and try again.

Cowboys mend fences. A good principle for everyone. Mend fences at home, at work, in all the arenas of our lives.

Cowboys get the gate. If two cowboys riding in a pickup come to a closed gate, the one not driving is usually the one designated to get the gate - or open it. As with cowboys, the gates, the opportunities we come to, aren't going to open themselves.

Cowboys know that life isn't always exciting. The cowboy's job can often be as boring as anyone else's. Life doesn't always have to be exciting. We need those routine days to help us get our bearings, set our directions, and prepare us for the times when all hell breaks loose.

Cowboys tip their hat. A well-mannered cowboy invariably tips or removes his hat when he meets a woman. It's a polite gesture, a reflection of courtesy and respect. Good manners are a sign of strength, not weakness.

Cowboys need time alone. We all need a little time alone with our thoughts, our dreams, our priorities, our values.

Cowboys are comfortable in the saddle. The saddle is

the cowboy's office. He may not be comfortable in all social situations, but in the saddle he is at home and confident. All of us have our comfort zones, where we are at our best. We should be careful in judging people's competence outside of their preferred environment.

Cowboys have common sense. They haven't learned their trade from books. They've learned it on the job and from each other. A cowboy has to be able to think on his feet – or in the saddle. Common sense is essential on the ranch – and everywhere else.

Cowboys understand their customers. Cowboys acquire what is called "cow sense" or "horse sense." That is, they learn to think like their customers (cattle) and their partners (horses). They also know what their bosses expect from them. Whatever business or endeavor we're in, we will be more successful if we can understand the points of view and expectations of our customers, our fellow workers, and our bosses.

Cowboys wear different hats. A cowboy might have a favorite work hat and another hat for going out on the town. A felt hat for fall, a straw hat for summer. Some cowboys even prefer caps, which don't cost nearly as much as custom hats. We all wear different hats in our various roles in life – parent, spouse, teacher, friend, voter, customer, worker. We are not just one personality wearing the same hat all the time but complicated individuals who cannot be easily labeled.

Cowboys see the big picture. The view from a bluff, a cliff, or a mesa reminds us of the vastness and richness and wonder of the world around us. It also puts our petty worries, grievances, jealousies, and pretensions into perspective.

Cowboys watch the sun rise. A sunrise on the range – or anywhere else – calls our attention to the new day that lies before us – a day full of opportunities as well as challenges, surprises as well as routine tasks.

Cowboys appreciate the sunset. Sunset on the plains offers a spectacular array of colors signaling the winding down of a workday. It also suggests a moment to reflect on the pluses and minuses of the day: feeling a sense of gratitude in whatever accomplishments have come our way; learning from the failures we may have encountered; and perhaps finding a little humility in the fact that no one is perfect.

Cowboys know the territory. Working cowboys know the terrain, the geography, the peaks and valleys of their ranch. Whatever our line of work, it is essential that we get to know the territory – not just the physical territory but the people, the language, the equipment, the inner workings of the job.

Cowboys have their own hall of fame. The National Cowboy Hall of Fame in Oklahoma City is an impressive tribute to the men and women who helped establish the West as an integral part of America's cultural heritage. If you talked to individual cowboys, however, they probably could tick off a few names of people they have ridden with or worked for, people they respect, who they would place in their own personal hall of honor. We all have those unwritten halls of fame – people who have made a difference in our lives. Who is in yours?

Cowboys enjoy the ride. And so should we all.

Strictly Fiction

Most of what I write would be labeled non-fiction. In other words, it's more or less true, although even non-fiction can be a bit subjective. The way I remember a story may not be exactly the way you remember it. The way I interpret a situation or an issue could be very different than how someone else might view it.

What follows in the next section are a few pieces that are strictly fiction. They are figments of my imagination. There may be a grain of truth in there somewhere, or not. The characters aren't real; they are made up.

The first piece, "The Toothpaste Gourmet," is a children's story that is a grandchild's favorite, followed by another story for young readers.

I'm not sure what I was drinking when I wrote "Talking Heads." You may wonder as well.

Four stories are from my one book of fiction, a collection of pieces about the good-hearted people who reside in the small fictional town of *Coleman Springs USA*. I like to say that the book has no sex, no violence, no bad language, and no plot! (It hasn't been a best-seller.)

Finally, the longest story (by far), is "Tex Starr for Governor," which pokes fun at nearly everything about the political process.

The inspiration for this story was probably Kinky Friedman's gubernatorial quest in 2006, but Tex Starr is quite a bit weirder than Kinky, if you can believe that. But maybe not any weirder than some previous and existing political figures I won't name.

The Toothpaste Gourmet

A Children's Story

My little brother is a little peculiar. He actually likes to brush his teeth.

No, that's not quite right. He *loves* to brush his teeth.

I've never known another boy who loves to brush his teeth. I certainly don't. My mom has to remind me several times every morning before I go to school and every night before I go to bed to brush my teeth.

"Have you brushed your teeth?" she yells up the stairs.

"Just a minute," I yell back.

A few minutes later she will come upstairs and say, "Don't forget to brush your teeth."

"Just a minute," I say.

I always brush them. Well, *almost* always. I know I need to and that it's good for me. But it's just not something that I look forward to, you know?

But my brother, Luke, now that's a different story.

Luke brushes his teeth the very first thing when he gets up in the morning.

After breakfast, he brushes them again.

He even takes his toothbrush to school in a special pouch so he can brush his teeth after lunch. I don't know of another single kid in school who does that. Well, maybe some *girls* do, but no boys that I know. Luke does.

First thing when we get home, Luke runs upstairs and brushes his teeth.

First thing after supper, yep – he brushes his teeth.

After his bath, before he puts on his pajamas, he brushes his teeth.

You're not going to believe this, but if he wakes up in the middle of the night, he will brush his teeth. I've seen him.

Of course, I asked him why he brushes his teeth so often. You know what he said?

"Because I like the taste of toothpaste." That's what he said.

And it's not just one flavor of toothpaste, either. Me, I stick with one brand and one flavor. But Luke, he likes to try all different types of brands and flavors.

My dad calls him the Toothpaste Gourmet. Dad just shakes his head and laughs. He can't believe it either.

Mom, she's just happy that she doesn't have to yell at both her boys to brush their teeth. Once she even scolded Luke to *stop* brushing his teeth.

We were eating supper, and Luke ate something that he didn't like, which was pretty unusual, too, because Luke likes to eat a lot of different types of food – like even spinach and squash and stuff like that.

Whatever it was that he didn't like, he *really* didn't like. He jumped up from the table and ran to the bathroom and started brushing his teeth.

That upset my mom. She told him to come back to the

table right now and finish his supper.

"I just had to get the taste out of my mouth," he said when he came back smelling like peppermint. "Please pass the spinach."

Luke, he's kind of weird, but one thing I'll say for him: He sure has nice teeth.

One Good Arm

I had never really thought about how lucky I am to have two good arms and two good legs until I got to know Billy Shadwick.

Billy didn't go to my school. We went to the same church, but we really didn't talk much. He had his friends, and I had mine. He was just that kid with the bad arm.

His left arm was normal, but his right arm was only about half as long as it should be. I heard someone say it was a "withered" arm. It didn't seem to bother Billy all that much. He was always laughing and cutting up with his friends. He seemed normal to me, except for the arm.

I did notice that he had more strength in his one good arm than most boys in either of their arms. He could beat nearly everyone in arm wrestling – well, in *left-handed* arm wrestling, of course.

Billy and I were eleven the year I got to know him. Our church – St. Thomas – had a team in the Church Youth Basketball League for boys twelve and under. Unlike some churches, we didn't recruit players outside our church. Unlike some churches, our team wasn't very good.

Our team consisted of the boys who actually attended St. Thomas. Billy and I were two of the eight boys who showed up for the first practice. Coach Lassiter said we would learn a lot about basketball, we would play hard, and we would have a good time. And we did.

Billy was always the first one at practice and the last one to leave. He wasn't a very good player because of his bad arm - and because he couldn't run very fast. One of his legs was a little shorter than the other.

Billy would be shooting the basketball when the rest of us would get there. He didn't make many, but he kept shooting. When practice was over, he would keep shooting after we had all left. His parents would stand and watch him shoot until Coach Lassiter said it was time to lock the gym.

Billy had a basketball goal in his driveway at home, and he told me he tried to practice at least one hour every afternoon. Sometimes two. Three or four hours on Saturday. He loved basketball.

We lost our first game 15-6 and our second one 19-7. I scored a goal in the first game but not the second. Billy Shadwick sat on the bench most of the game. When he did get in the game, he took a few shots but didn't make any of them.

Our third game was against Western Heights Church, one of the teams that brought in kids from the neighborhood to play. They said it was part of their "ministry" to the neighborhood. We said they were "ministering" especially to kids who could play basketball.

That day two of our players were sick with the flu, but the flu bug had also hit out at Western Heights. We had six players show up. They only had five.

Billy Shadwick sat on the bench to start the game. He

substituted for me for a few minutes in the second quarter and went in for Mark Parrick for a few minutes in the third quarter.

Meanwhile, we were staying close to Western Heights. At the half the score was 7-6, and at the end of the third quarter we were tied 10-10. Mark had scored six points, I had two, and Jason Richard had two.

Western Heights went ahead 12-10, but Mark scored again to make it 12-12. They kept missing shots. We kept missing shots. And then the worst thing happened. Mark got called for his fifth foul, which meant he had fouled out. We were doomed.

Billy Shadwick came in. Western Heights missed the first free throw but made the second. 13-12. We got the ball, and I thought I had a good shot, but it rolled around the rim and dropped out. Western Heights went down and made another basket. 15-12. There were only fifteen seconds left in the game.

The Western Heights players were all over us when we tried to take the ball down the court. They put two of their best players guarding me. The only player not guarded was Billy.

Billy got the ball and started dribbling down the court. One of their players came over and tried to take the ball away, but he fouled.

Billy would get to shoot two free throws, but there were only five seconds left in the game. Even if he made both of them, we were still beaten.

Coach Lassiter called a time out. "Billy," he said, "after you make the first shot, here's what I want you to do…"

Sure enough, Billy made the first free throw. 15-13. On the second shot, he threw the ball as hard as he could against the rim. It bounced right back to him, and he shot again. But this time it was for two points. The ball hit the backboard and bounced right through the net just as the buzzer sounded. We had tied them 15-15.

In the overtime period, two of the Western Heights players fouled out, leaving them only three on the court. I scored two baskets and Jason made a free throw, and we won 20-15.

After we finished celebrating, Coach Lassiter called us together. He was holding the basketball from the game, and on it in big black ink he had written 20-15.

"Boys," he said, "all of you played your best. You played hard and you didn't give up. I'm very proud of you. I want to present this game ball to the player we would all agree was the star of the game —Billy Shadwick."

Billy took the ball and ran back on the court. As we watched, he took one more shot and then another and another and another and another and another – until he finally made one.

Then he smiled and walked out with his parents, holding the game ball in his one good arm.

Intruders

She awoke suddenly and sat straight up in bed.

What was that noise? How long had she been asleep? What time was it anyway? What *day* was it?

Slowly it began to come back to her. She had dragged in from another grueling eleven-hour day – her third this week – and just flopped onto the bed, not even taking time to get out of her dress.

Or bothering to lock the door, she realized! What was that noise?

She looked at the digital clock on her bedside table. She had been asleep a little less than an hour. Or had it been thirteen hours? Could she have slept all night and now it was the next morning?

She listened carefully for the sound that had obviously startled her from slumber. Above the constant city noises that a Manhattan resident becomes accustomed to, she thought she heard a murmur in the living room. She was sure of it.

But one of her roommates had left yesterday for a long weekend in The Hamptons, and the other one was down in Florida on a business trip.

Now she was wide awake. It was still Friday. It was dark outside. And someone was in her apartment!

Her eyes adjusted to the dark room. She reached for her purse on the floor and quietly fumbled for the can of pepper spray she always kept ready for such an emergency.

Should she stay in her bedroom and hope the intruder would take whatever he was after and leave? Or should she investigate?

Maybe it wasn't anyone after all. Maybe just wind noise.

What was that! She knew she heard movement. She thought she heard another whisper. Could there be more than one person?

Was that a chair moving across the floor? Were they taking her furniture? Not her grandmother's chair, the only piece of furniture she had brought with her from Texas. By God, they weren't going to get that chair without suffering for it!

Silently she swung out of bed, grasped the spray, and charged through the door, screaming at the top of her voice the way she had learned in her kick boxing class.

"Aiiiiiiiiiieeeeeeeee!"

Four startled girlfriends watched as she lunged into the room, almost tripping over the coffee table where they had arranged plates, cups, napkins, two bottles of champagne, and a birthday cake.

Talking Heads

If those heads could talk, I was thinking, I bet they'd have some stories to tell.

I was in one of those mountain lodges, the kind with the mounted heads on the wall. Heads of majestic creatures hunted and slain. Trophies testifying to the courage and prowess of Real Men.

But this place was different. You could tell right off. It was the mounted heads. There were ten of them in all, and I couldn't take my eyes off them. Their eyes seemed to follow me as I walked over and began reading the inscriptions.

George V. "Antlers" Anderson, 1902-1971.

"Known for the antlers he wore as a decoy to attract deer and elk. Killed in a hunting accident when his partner mistook him for an elk."

Greg "Mountain Man" Bischner, 1949-1974.

"Too cheap to stay at hunting lodges, he claimed to prefer roughing it. Camped out sometimes for weeks at a time. Froze to death during the '74 blizzard."

Andrew M. "Backpack" Carver, 1918-1976.

"Liked to boast about how far he walked every day and the rough terrain he mastered. Constantly challenged other hunters to keep up with him. Suffered heart attack while tying his shoes; died instantly."

Dr. Spencer "Indy" Long, 1926-1979.

"Race car driver before becoming cardiologist. Drove off a cliff on his way to the hunting lodge."

Michael R. "Ace" Counse, 1964-1983.

"Astounded fellow hunters by winning poker pot with a five-ace hand. Shot by another player who accused him of cheating."

Kevin "Red" McDouglas, 1955-1983.

"Fiery temper, especially when losing at poker. Tracked down and shot while trying to escape after killing poker cheat in cold blood."

Raymond "Satellite" Tillsdale, 1917-1986.

"Not much of a hunter. A dedicated channel surfer, he once accessed 233 different programs in an hour on the hunting lodge TV. Bored himself to death."

Dr. J. Lamar "Prexy" Barrington, 1935-1990.

"University president. Impeccable dresser and connoisseur of fine wine and continental cuisine, but also loved the rugged outdoors. Choked on tough piece of meat during dinner."

J.V. "Junior" Riggins, 1927-1993.

"Rarely known to be sober. Claimed he could outdrink any hunter alive and seemed determined to prove it - often. Passed out drunk and hit his head on stone floor of lodge bar; never regained consciousness."

The tenth mounted head really grabbed my attention. It was MINE.

I walked over to it. My face was flushed and I was burning up. Then suddenly I could feel myself getting cold. I began to tremble. The shaking became uncontrollable as I strained to read the caption.

"Honey, wake up! You've been tossing and talking in your sleep, and you've kicked off all the covers. What's the matter? You look like you've seen a ghost."

Pappy Died

My friend Taylor Campbell, our local doctor and my neighbor, came by early this morning. He just wanted to talk. He was almost in tears.

"I had to have Pappy put to sleep this morning," Taylor said.

No wonder he was so sad.

"Oh, I'm so sorry," I told Taylor. "I know how much you loved Pappy."

Pappy is Taylor's cocker spaniel. He's had Pappy more years than he's had his second wife, Jill.

"It just got to where Pappy couldn't function anymore," Taylor said. "Jill and I would put out food, and he would barely touch it. He just lay there, hardly moving.

"When he did go outside yesterday morning, he wouldn't come back in. I think he went outside to die. We picked him up and carried him back in the house, but this morning he hadn't moved from where we laid him. He was barely breathing.

"I could tell he had been in pain for quite a while. I just couldn't bring myself to let him go. But this morning, I told Jill I was going to take him to Dr. Waters and have him put out of his misery. It just seemed like the humane thing to do.

"Dr. Waters – Will – was very sensitive. He said it would be better if I just let him handle it. I suppose I could have stayed with Pappy and held him, and I kind of wanted to, but Will thought it would be best if I didn't. So I gave Pappy a kiss and then I cried. I sat outside in the waiting room.

"It didn't take long. Will wrapped up Pappy in a blanket and put him in a cardboard box with a lid, like a coffin I suppose. Will gave me a hug and I carried Pappy's box out to the car.

"I went home and dug a grave and buried Pappy in the back yard. I don't think I'll put up a tombstone or anything, but somehow I feel better knowing that Pappy is still close by. I'll probably plant some wildflowers on his grave. I think he would like that."

Taylor was quiet for a moment. Neither of us said anything. Then he said, "I really appreciate the peaceful way in which Pappy died, and it certainly made me stop and think about how much more humane we are with our pets' final days than we are with the people we love.

"When my father had Alzheimer's, I know he wanted to go ahead and die. He even said so at one point before the Alzheimer's got so bad, and even after he couldn't talk, I knew that he would have preferred to save himself and everyone else the misery of continuing to live with such a debilitating condition.

"Of course, we couldn't do for him what I did for Pappy. And I know there are all kinds of ethical and moral ramifications involving euthanasia, in addition to the legal issues, and I am sworn as a physician to view life as sacred. But I have to wonder, which is more humane – which is really more sacred in the long run - to let people continue to suffer when there is no hope for recovery or improvement, or to do what I did this morning with Pappy?"

"Taylor," I said, "I agree with you, but I doubt that is an issue you and I can decide here today."

"I know," he said, "but maybe we at least ought to raise the questions. I'm going to write a letter to someone. I don't know who, and I doubt it will make any difference, but I will feel better getting my thoughts down on paper."

"You do that, Taylor," I said.

Later that day I sent a small check to the regional animal shelter in Pappy's name. That evening, my wife and I talked about what Taylor had said.

"I would certainly rather go like Pappy did," she said.

"I would, too," I said, "but don't go getting any ideas!"

Postcard Minister

Lacy Curry sent another postcard to the president of the United States today.

Every few months she writes a postcard to the president. Not a protest or anything, and not necessarily agreeing with him either.

She just writes something like, "Dear Mr. President, You have a tough job, and I just want to say thank you."

Or, "Dear Mr. President, I will be praying for you."

Or, "Dear Mr. President, May you be blessed with wisdom and grace."

Or, "Dear Mr. President, We are counting on you."

Lacy has been sending postcards like that to the White House since Eisenhower was president. She has written them all, about four or five times a year on average, whether she voted for them or not.

It started with an English assignment when Lacy was in high school. The teacher handed out three postcards to everyone in class and told them to write three people and say something encouraging to them.

Lacy chose her grandmother, who was barely able to see anymore, knowing someone would read it to her. Then she sent a card to a cousin, congratulating him on winning a blue ribbon for his trumpet solo. And then she decided to write President Eisenhower.

She was surprised to get a reply from the White House. So, a couple of months later, she wrote him again, and every so often after that while he was in office. When Kennedy became president, she continued her little hobby. Then Johnson, Nixon, Ford, Carter, Reagan, and each one since. They've all written her back, just standard, official White House replies at first, but eventually each president wrote her a personal letter saying how much they looked forward to receiving her kind words of encouragement.

She never tried to sway any of their views on any issue, figuring, "They are there and they have a lot more information than I do. I just want them to know that someone cares and appreciates the often-thankless job they have to do."

Even during a president's darkest days, she wrote messages like, "Dear Mr. President, May you have the strength to face these trying times." Or, "Dear Mr. President, May the Lord bless you and keep you all the day long."

Lacy moved here with her husband, Bob, when Johnson was president. As the town's postmaster, I got to know her right away, not just because she wrote to the president frequently, but also because she wrote a postcard to someone *every day*. At least one. You might say she has been one of my best customers through the years. I figure that she has probably sent fifteen to twenty thousand postcards in her lifetime. Or more.

Someone new moves to town, they get a postcard from Lacy welcoming them here. When kids she knows go off to college, she sends them a postcard after about a month, thinking they might be getting a little homesick by then. Anyone in town who needs cheering up will get a postcard from Lacy.

She calls it her "postcard ministry."

"It's just a little thing," she told me, "but it's a little thing that I can do."

Several years ago the Chamber of Commerce honored her as our Citizen of the Year. Appropriately, the next week, she received congratulatory postcards from nearly everyone in town.

He Could Fix Anything

"He could fix anything."

That's what they inscribed on Possum Johnson's tombstone.

Possum knew he was going to die for several weeks, and he had made his peace with the world. He also told his brother, Otis, what he wanted his tombstone to say. "Might as well say, 'He could fix anything.' That's what they'll all remember me for."

And that was true. It didn't matter if your washer or dryer had quit working, or your TV or air-conditioner had gone out, or something was wrong with your car or motorcycle or boat, Possum could fix it. I don't mean he would *try* to fix it. I mean he would fix it.

Oh, occasionally there would be something that would be beyond repair, but you usually knew that before Possum had to tell you. In that case, you would just tell him to get rid of it for you – but, of course, he didn't. He just tossed it somewhere in the back of his workshop, or in the back yard, and kept it for spare parts. Didn't matter if it was a refrigerator or a radio or a computer. Eventually, he found some use for at least part of the machine.

Now computers were kind of a challenge for Possum at first. But it wasn't too long before he got the hang of them. A computer, after all, is just a machine, and there wasn't a machine alive that could outsmart Possum Johnson for very long. He fixed many a cell phone and fax machine, too.

We're really going to miss Possum around here. There aren't many people in a town who are actually irreplaceable, as much as we might like to think we are. But Possum – well, I doubt we'll ever find anyone like him again.

You're probably wondering how Possum got his nickname, and I'm afraid I don't know. He's been Possum for as long as I've known him, and I guess I've known him pretty much all his life. They started calling him Possum when he was a toddler, and it just stuck with him.

The obituary notice in the city paper listed him as Possum Johnson. At his funeral Elliott Sanders, the pastor of The Church of the Living Word, called him Possum. He said when Possum was ordained as an elder in the church, he asked to be ordained as Brother Possum.

"It sounded like something from a children's story," the pastor said, and everyone laughed.

Brother Possum's primary responsibility at The Church of the Living Word was, naturally, to fix things.

"There's no telling how much money Brother Possum saved us over the years," the preacher said. "And he always did it so willingly, so cheerfully. I told him one time that his ability to fix things was truly a gift from God, and he laughed and said, 'Oh, preacher, anyone can do what I do.' And I told him, 'That's how you know it is a gift from God, when something comes so naturally to you.' He thought about that a minute and said, 'Well, I'll be danged.'"

The funeral procession from the church to Rosemont Cemetery stretched for at least half a mile. Ironically, two cars overheated along the way and had to be parked on the side of the road.

Possum Johnson would have had them running in no time. Possum Johnson. "He could fix anything."

A Wonderful Life

Our town is different today. People are going about their daily routine, but it is as if a cloud has descended and we are all in a daze or a fog. There is no laughter, no joy, no small talk. It doesn't seem appropriate.

When tragedy strikes a small town, where everyone knows everyone else, it affects the entire town. No one is immune. We all feel the pain.

We know we will be a long time recovering. Life in our town will never be quite the same. Eventually, we suppose, life will resume its normal pace and people will smile again and will find meaning and purpose in what we do. But it will not be the same.

We all want to say something, we want to do something, we want to make some sense of it and give our friends some relief from the overwhelming sorrow that surrounds and penetrates and engulfs them.

And, like our friends, we want to remember. We cling to the idea that life is a gift, and we remember that the candle, which has been snuffed out so abruptly, burned brightly and illuminated our lives, even if ever so briefly.

Rainey McDermond was, without question, the most beautiful girl in her class when she graduated from high school here almost twenty years ago. She had a natural beauty that needed no artificial enhancement. She did not flaunt it;

if anything, she did all she could to play down the fact how gorgeous she really was.

As a child she was quite the tomboy. She liked to collect frogs and lizards and rocks, go fishing in Blue Pond, organize neighborhood campouts in her back yard, and challenge all the boys to a foot race which she knew she would win.

But there was no hiding the fact, especially when she entered high school, that she was beautiful. And her smile and her laugh and her easy-going charm drew people to her. She made friends easily, and she made friends abundantly.

Not just among her peers either. Old men and women, and little girls and boys, and parents of her high school pals, found themselves drawn like a magnet into her circle.

No wonder she was voted not only most beautiful, but most likely to succeed. She went off to college, majored in elementary education, taught second grade, married a young preacher in North Carolina, and gave birth to two beautiful children – a daughter, with red hair like her mother, and a son who, it quickly became apparent, had inherited his mother's athletic ability.

And then, about a year ago, during a routine exam the doctor found a lump. And then another and another. The doctors did everything they could, but in the end there wasn't anything left to do.

Rainey and her husband prayed like they had never prayed before. When it became apparent that their prayers would not be answered in the way they had hoped, they began making plans for life for the family after she was gone.

Her parents, Kevan and Paige McDermond, were devastated. They went to North Carolina to be with their daughter and to help with the grandchildren. Friends here at home sent cards and letters and numerous prayers their way. A fund was organized to help with medical costs.

Rainey fought with everything she had. "Every day," she told her mother, "is a gift from God. I know you have taught me that all my life, but now I see it more clearly and feel it more deeply."

She was in and out of the hospital several times. Finally, the last time, she knew it was the last time. She asked her dad to go to her favorite bakery and buy a big chocolate cake. And then she threw one last party for the nurses and aides and doctors who had been so kind to her.

That was a week ago Friday. She held on for three more days and said all her good-byes. She told her husband, "I am the luckiest woman in the world to have been married to you and to have had two wonderful children. I have truly had, as the movie said, a wonderful life. Thank you."

They had the funeral at their church in North Carolina but also held a memorial service for her at the Baptist church here. Her husband spoke briefly, and so did her father and one of her friends from high school. The congregation sang, at her request, "When We All Get to Heaven."

The Rev. Andrew Baker got up to deliver a sermon, but, instead of speaking, he had everyone stand and hold hands and sing "Blest Be the Tie." Everyone was hugging, crying, remembering, and praying.

And two days later, we still are.

Tex Starr for Governor

Howdy. I'm Tex Starr, and I'm running for governor.

Of Texas, of course. You don't think someone named Tex would be running for governor of, say, New Jersey or Minnesota, do you?

I'm running as an independent, not as an R or a D. I like some things about the R's and some things about the D's, but mostly I find that both the R's and the D's get too hung up on being R's and D's instead of trying to do what's best for everybody.

As an independent, I figure, in some ways I have to get along with everybody, and in other ways I don't have to get along with anybody.

Here's the bottom line: I don't really care whether I'm elected or not. I mean, yeah, I want to be elected, but it's not so important to me that I will do anything to *get* elected. If I get elected, great. If I don't, hail, it's not the end of the world.

Next time I might run for president.

The First Family

The first thing a candidate is expected to do is introduce his family. So I will.

My family includes me, my wife, our son, and our daughter. Now, you might laugh when you see our names all put together – or you might stand up and salute. We're about as Texas as you're gonna find.

My name really is Tex Starr. Now, it wasn't the name I was born with. I was born "Joe Beckworth Starr." But when I was in college, in Ohio, people kept calling me "Tex," and I came to like it. So I had my name officially changed to "Tex Starr."

I didn't change it just so I could run for governor. I've been "Tex Starr" for pretty near twenty years. But, hail, I figured it wouldn't hurt if I ever *did* decide to run for governor, or county commissioner for that matter.

Enough about me. Let's talk about the rest of my family.

My wife is TexAnna Starr. We met in college. I was from Texas. She was from Texas. They called me Tex. They called her Anna, because that was her name, Anna Jessup Walker.

We hit it off right away, and pretty soon we were talking about getting married. I told her my plans and how I wanted to officially change my name to "Tex Starr." She laughed. Then she said, "And I should be TexAnna." You can see why we fell in love.

So we went to the courthouse and changed our names. I became Tex Starr and she became TexAnna Walker. Then, a few months later, when we got married – in a church in Texas, of course – we became Mr. and Mrs. Tex Starr, or if you prefer, Tex and TexAnna Starr.

Then came children: a boy, Tex Junior, who is now eleven years old; and a girl, age eight, named Texette, a pretty unusual name, I realize, except in our family. She plans to be governor herself someday.

So there we are – The First Family of Texas, we call ourselves – Tex, TexAnna, Tex Junior, and Texette.

I just know you're already warming up to us. You're thinking – a family as nutty as this is bound to be taken seriously in Texas politics.

Exactly what I hoped you would say.

Don't Write Like You Talk

One thing I need to make clear up front. I don't write the way I talk.

I wanted to. When I first started issuing press releases about my candidacy, I dropped all the g's off the endings of words, like endings. I would have said endin's. And when I said, "One thing I need to make clear," I would have written it "One thang I need to make clear."

But my new PR gal said I can't (or cain't) do that. I have to write in English, not colloquial Texan, or people won't take me seriously.

Hail, I told her, they're not going to take me seriously anyway. Still, she insisted that I write in English.

Now one thing (thang) I did insist on with the PR gal is that, in order to keep my language clean, I would be allowed to say "hail" instead of "hell" when I needed to make a point with emphasis.

In Texas, people understand that "hail" has two different meanings. It can be a substitute for a mild profanity, or it can describe stuff falling from the sky during a storm. In either case, and in spite of how it looks, it's a two-syllable word – "HEY-ul." Hail.

How Hard Could It Be?

We've had independent candidates run for governor of Texas before. They didn't do all that well.

So, what's to say that I will? Well, first of all, the people may be more fed up now than they were before. Should be.

One of the more recent independent candidates – who also had a great name, Kinky – had several pretty good slogans. One was, "How Hard Could It Be?" – an apt description of what it means to be governor. The governor in Texas doesn't really have a lot of power, or all that much to do, but he has a lot of influence, or thinks he does. Or she. We've had two women governors.

Actually, I've found the "How Hard Could It Be?" slogan to be applicable to a lot of situations. When I'm in a group and someone comes up with a very good and very workable and practical idea, invariably someone else will whine about how they can't (cain't) do this or the other, how this or the other hasn't worked before, and so on. And I like to say, "Well, as Kinky says, how hard could it be?"

Kinky also had a bumper sticker slogan that read, "Why the hell not?" And I think that's why he didn't win. People, especially older people, are offended by the use of "hell" if not in context with sinners going there. Had Kinky said, "Why the hail not?" he might've won.

Well, I can't (cain't) ride on Kinky's coattails, and wouldn't want to. He lost, after all. So I've come up with my own slogans.

"I'm not as stupid as I look."

"I'm not as stupid as I sound."

"We've had stupid governors before."

OK, maybe I need to work on these a little more. My PR gal says they don't quite have the ring I'm looking for.

My Qualifications

OK, big guy, you're thinking, what qualifies you to be governor of the great state of Texas?

Well, I have to confess that I haven't been a wrestler (rassler), a movie star, a country singer, an oil man, a TV preacher, a football coach, or a baseball executive. Nor have I ever served a term in either prison or political office. So much for traditional qualifications.

Several things, I think, qualify me to be your next governor:

I'm alive.

I live in Texas.

I'm not a felon.

I have a great family, as you've already seen.

And I am filthy rich.

That last point is probably the most important. You see, I have enough money to run an expensive, all-out campaign.

But here's the deal: I don't plan to spend much of it. I didn't become rich by foolishly throwing money away.

I made my money the old-fashioned way. I inherited it. I've

spent my whole life – well, the years since college anyway – in the family business, and it hasn't gone broke yet. Besides my good looks, wit, and charm, one of the things that attracted a beauty like TexAnna to marry me was that my family was rolling in dough.

So was hers, though that had nothing to do with my decision to court, propose to, and marry her.

Anyway, our families saw our marriage as more of a merger than a marriage. But we didn't. For us, it was true love. Still is.

It's true that money doesn't buy happiness, although I never heard my parents say that. But money does buy elections.

Still, I want to make it clear, I'm not out to buy this election. I probably could, but that would be wrong. I don't want to be governor because I'm rich. I want to be governor because I'm nuts.

Interview with the Candidate

Not long after I announced my candidacy for governor, I was interviewed by Victoria Z. Hesterman, political editor of the *Dallas Daily Gazette, Journal & Free Voice*. I think we covered most of the substantive issues of the campaign. Here is the edited version of our conversation that was published:

Are you serious about running for governor?
I've never been more serious about anything in my life.

Have you ever been serious about anything in your life?

Not really.

If elected, what would be the first thing you would do?

I would look at my wife, TexAnna, and say, "What the hail do we do now?"

And then what?

Then I would hug my daughter, Texette, and high-five my son, Tex Junior.

OK, and then?

Then we would all go out to eat at our favorite pizza place.

I mean, what would you start working on, what plans would you make?

Well, I suppose I would have to start going through my campaign promises and try to figure out which ones to keep.

Are you saying you won't keep all the promises you make in the campaign?

I wouldn't want to give politics a bad name.

So, let me be sure I'm getting this right. You're saying that during the campaign you will be making promises you really don't expect to keep?

Oh, I expect to keep them. I just don't think anyone else expects me to keep them, and I wouldn't want to let them down.

Why do you want to be governor anyway?

I want to be famous.

But, I mean, what do you want to accomplish?

As little as possible.

Then why should anyone vote for you, if you're going into the campaign saying you're not going to do much?

That's exactly why they ought to vote for me. I promise not to do very much. You want limited government? Hail, I'm your guy.

Is that a promise you expect to keep?

It's at the top of the list. I've made a career out of doing nothing. The voters can trust me to uphold that tradition when I become governor.

Do you really expect to win?

No, but wouldn't it be a hoot if I did?

If you don't win, what will you do next?

I might run for president.

Why?

That would make me even more famous.

It's been written in the press that you have so much money that you can afford to run for governor without taking any contributions. Is that right?

Not only that. I won't even accept bribes. Well, not small ones, anyway.

But what about campaign contributions? What if someone offered to give you a million dollars?

Oh, I thought you were talking about one-dollar or ten-dollar donations. Hail, of course, I'd take a million dollars. I'm not as stupid as I look.

So, you can be bought by the rich special interests?

Not at all. I said I would take their money, not that I would do what they want.

Wouldn't it at least appear that you had been bought?

As my granddaddy used to say, "All politicians can be bought. The honest ones are the ones that stay bought." So, I suppose, I wouldn't be an honest politician because I wouldn't stay bought.

Did your granddaddy hold public office?

No, he was a lobbyist.

Getting on the Ballot

The first challenge for an independent candidate is to collect the required number of signatures to get on the ballot.

In Texas, where they really don't want independent candidates to foul up the one-party system, they make it very hard. You have to get somewhere around a bazillion signatures from people who *haven't voted* in either the R or D primary, haven't been to prison, and have the IQ of at least a live goldfish.

When I told people (mostly my cousins and what few friends I have) that I was gonna run for governor, they said in unison, "How will you get enough signatures to get on the ballot?"

Actually, it was easy. The signatures are collected. I have already qualified. I'm on the ballot.

What I did was this. I gave away a house. Not just any house, but a double-wide. I figured if you want to get to the people, speak their language. So I had a drawing.

Anyone could sign up at no charge. All they had to do

was (a) be a registered voter who (b) didn't vote in the R or D primary and (c) signed a petition nominating me as an independent candidate for governor. (Well, they didn't actually *have* to sign the petition because that might be considered that I had offered them a bribe, which of course I am philosophically opposed to. But, just to be nice, they signed it anyway.)

Lines formed all over the state. I had the signatures in three hours.

And one lucky registered voter (I won't tell you who, out of respect for her privacy, but her initials are Eula Bell Krumpsett) now has her very own double-wide, and I even threw in a subscription to the Double Wide Edition of *Southern Homes Magazine*.

Is this a great state or what?

I'm thinking of trying (tryin') the same thing (thang) in the general election. Everbody who says they voted for me gets their name in a drawing for another double-wide. (Winner of the first drawing isn't eligible.) To improve the odds and boost the Texas economy, I might even give away two more double-wides.

Of course, in Texas, voting is done in secret, so how would I know who was a legitimate contender for the drawing and who was illegitimate, meaning they voted R or D?

Simple. I'd just ask. You got to be able to trust the people, don't you?

Campaign Advertising

My Uncle Clyde had a chain of locally-owned grocery stores, SuperSuperMart, in a large Texas city back in the '90s (the 1990s).

Every Wednesday he took out a full-page color ad in the *Large City News-Advocate-Times-Inquirer* advertising his specials on dog food, soft drinks, green beans, toilet paper, or whatever he needed to move that week.

A new publisher was brought in from Up North by the *Large City News-Advocate*, etc., and he immediately declared that the advertising rates at the local newspaper were way too low and would, henceforth, be increased by 9.25 percent. Never mind that the number of subscribers to the *News-Advocate-Times-Inquirer* had declined by 44 percent in the past six years and no one under 50 ever picked it up.

Uncle Clyde tried to reason with the publisher, who had his MBA from Very Prestigious U. framed on his wall and who informed Uncle Clyde that, according to the Institute of Newspaper-Funded Research, the ad rates for the *N-A-T-I* were in the lower 95 percentile of newspapers in their (declining) circulation category.

Uncle Clyde said, fine, he couldn't quibble with research and he certainly didn't want to quit advertising. He would be happy to sign a new long-term contract at the new ad rate. The publisher took pride in winning the confrontation. Uncle Clyde then asked if the new rate would cover whatever size ads he wished to run. The publisher said it would. Could he run his ad every day?, Uncle Clyde asked. Of course, the publisher beamed. For the next three years?, Uncle Clyde asked. Absolutely, said the overjoyed publisher.

The next Wednesday, readers picked up the paper and found a two-inch ad that read:

"The newspaper has jacked up the price of its ads. But at **SuperSuperMart**, you still get the same great low prices. Come see us for details."

On Thursday: "**SuperSuperMart** can only afford a small newspaper ad so we can still afford to give you great low prices. Come see for yourself."

On Friday: "**SuperSuperMart** could pay more for ads, or we could pass along the savings to you. We choose you."

On Saturday: "Somebody's paying for those expensive newspaper ads. At **SuperSuperMart**, it isn't you."

On Sunday: "If you want expensive newspaper ads, look somewhere else. If you want low prices, come to **SuperSuperMart**."

On Monday: "Every day we have a little-bitty ad to remind you of our little-bitty markup at **SuperSuperMart**."

On Tuesday: "**SuperSuperMart** has too many great prices to list in this tiny ad. Check us out."

And so on. Pretty soon a furniture store switched from full-page color ads to the two-inch approach. Then a major department store followed suit. Then a hearing aid provider. After two weeks, the publisher called Uncle Clyde and offered him the old ad rate if he would resume his full-page color ads.

Uncle Clyde told him what he could do with his ad rate.

I tell this lengthy story to explain that I'm following my Uncle Clyde's example in my campaign. In the next few weeks leading up to Election Day, you will be seeing a series of teeny ads every day in every major and minor daily newspaper in Texas. They aren't cheap, but they're not as expensive as TV, and not nearly as offensive either. And even though newspaper readership may be older, at least those people vote!

I won't be able to get much of a message in a one or two-inch ad, but – hail! – I don't have all that much to say anyway. Plus, let's be honest, it's more than most politicians have to offer if you stripped away the bull-plop. And it's as much as most voters want to read anyway.

A few examples:

"I won't make any promises I can't keep. In other words, I won't make any promises at all. **Tex Starr for Governor.**"

"Government should do less. I've been doing less all my life. **Tex Starr for Governor.**"

"I may be stupid, but I'm rich and don't need to steal. **Tex Starr for Governor.**"

"You deserve a better governor, but it doesn't look like you're going to have that choice this year. **Tex Starr for Governor.**"

"Ask your friends to vote for me. You'll probably have to make new friends. **Tex Starr for Governor.**"

"I have more money than I do sense. Just like the government. **Tex Starr for Governor.**"

"Kick the rascals out. Elect a new rascal. **Tex Starr for**

Governor."

"My campaign is not a joke. State government is. **Tex Starr for Governor.**"

"I'm not perfect. So if you are, you should vote for someone else. **Tex Starr for Governor.**"

"My wife TexAnna, my son Tex Junior, and my daughter Texette would like you to visit us if we become the First Family of Texas. Bring your own lunch. **Tex Starr for Governor.**"

Maybe I'll also put these ads on FaceTwit or whatever you call it.

Be Sure to Vote

See you at the polls. Vote for me and maybe you'll win a double-wide. Vote for the R or the D, and – hail! – that's all you'll be able to afford when they get through raising (raisin') your taxes!

Be sure to sign up for a bumper sticker and a yard sign with my new campaign slogan:

Tex Starr for Governor.
Less Is What We Need More Of.

My PR gal just throwed up her hands and quit. I probly didn't need her anyways. I'm plenty capable of writin' my own press releases and gettin' myself interviewed on TV.

It Could Be Verse

Poetry is kind of hard to define these days. There are so many types and styles of poems. My own definition is that a poem is a glimpse of truth expressed in a format in which each line communicates or suggests an idea or thought.

In many ways, poetry is a performance art. People who don't think they like poetry are often surprised when they hear a poet reading his or her poems. Most of the poems in this section, or scattered through the other sections of the book, are ones that I've read out loud to civic or church groups, study clubs, book festivals, family gatherings, etc., over the years and seem to have been well-received by the listeners.

Quite frankly, a lot of poems I come across just leave me wondering what the poet was trying to say. Why should we have to work so hard to try to understand what a poem is about?

I hope that's not the case with my poems. Some are humorous, some are serious, some tell a story, some are snapshots, and I've just mixed them up, not separating the funny ones from the serious ones because in life we are laughing one moment and reflecting or crying the next.

Please just read them, don't overanalyze them. This isn't English class.

A Day's Work

All I have to show
for my work today
are just these few lines

no new buildings built
no major deals made
no wayward souls saved

no mail delivered
no learning passed on
no cars or homes sold

no sick people healed
no courtroom drama
no fires extinguished

no mysteries solved
no startling insights
no blaring headlines

just these few lines but
that will have to do
until tomorrow

The Power of a Smile

Give the World a Smile
It's something anyone can do,
an adult or a child.
We all have it in our power
to give the world a smile.

A Smile and a Donut
The cheerful clerk
at the pastry shop
makes it her business
to sweeten the day
of everyone she meets.

Three Ways to Smile
Smile first.
Smile big.
Smile often.

Smiles Matter
You think that smiles
aren't important?
Just try living
a day without them.

Delivery with a Smile

Inspired by Andy, the UPS guy

He always has a smile on his face
and a cheerful greeting
for the customers on his route.

He calls everyone "my friend"
and as a result everyone
thinks of him the same way.

Entire courses in customer service
could be condensed into one day
of just following him around.

Seven Wonders

The wonder of today.

The wonder of life.

The wonder of beauty.

The wonder of nature.

The wonder of joy.

The wonder of love.

The wonder of you.

My Old Dog

She sleeps all day
She sleeps all night
She never barks
And wouldn't bite.

She's blind and deaf
Can barely stand
She only eats
Out of my hand.

My friend so true
These many years
God rest your soul
And dry my tears.

Each Raindrop

I listen with gratitude as the gentle rain
pitters and patters and waters
the thirsty vegetation around me.

I am reminded to be thankful –
not just for the rainfall in general,
but for each raindrop in particular.

That one – I don't know your name –
but you gave new life and new hope
to that dying brown blade of grass.

Oh, and you, named Joe or Bob or Mary,
your little insignificant drop by drop
nourished those lovely purple flowers.

And if it hadn't been for you, yes you,
your kind word at just the right moment,
I, too, would have wilted on the vine.

Pillows on the Bed

Evidently we men just don't understand
why a bed needs to be piled high with pillows.
It must be something about our male genes
that makes us think you only need one pillow
for every person who is sleeping in the bed,
not counting, of course, those for propping up
so you can watch TV.

What's the point of all those other pillows?
At night you take them off the bed
and pile them up somewhere in the room,
only to put them back on the bed
the next morning after the bed is made.
Seems kind of pointless, if you ask me,
but, of course, you didn't.

Not-So-Love Poems for Valentine's Day

These days, you know, most poems don't rhyme. You can just kind of go off and say whatever you want to and make a poem out of it. So you could probably write a poem yourself for that special someone in your life.

But before you do that, you might want to consider NOT just saying the first thing that pops into your head. Here are a few Valentine's Day poems you might NOT want to give to your sweetheart. I call them *"not-so-love poems."*

Every morning I wake up
And brush my teeth
And spit into the sink
And so this morning
I woke up and brushed my teeth
But before I spit into the sink
I remembered it was Valentine's Day
And I hadn't bought you a present
So I wrote you this poem -
Happy Valentine's Day

The first thing I think of every morning
Is all the things I have to do today.
The second thing I think of every morning
Is all the pills I need to take at the right time.
The third thing I think of every morning
Is what are we going to have for lunch and dinner.
And this morning the fourth thing I thought of -
Well, I should have thought of it earlier -
Is Happy Valentine's Day

We were both a lot younger back then
And we're a lot older now
But then and now
One thing has remained the same:
I still like to play golf and watch football
And you don't –
Happy Valentine's Day

♥ ♥ ♥

I wrote you this Valentine's poem
Instead of buying you a box of candy
Because you are on a diet -
Happy Valentine's Day

I wrote you this Valentine's poem
Instead of buying you flowers
Because they jack up the price so much
For a dozen roses around Valentine's Day
That it would be cheaper to take you to out
To a very nice and expensive dinner -
But it would be even cheaper
To write you this Valentine's poem –
Happy Valentine's Day

Roses are red
I am cheap
Here's a poem
You can keep
Instead of a rose
Which would just die
And so will I
But not today -
Happy Valentine's Day

Well, here's kind of a love poem, I guess. At least it has rhyme and rhythm:

♥ A Poem Instead of a Mink

When the sun doesn't sink
And the stars don't twink
And ice doesn't clink
And writers don't drink
And skunks don't stink
And chains don't link
And clothes don't shrink
And eyes don't blink
And light red isn't pink,
Maybe then you can think
That I have run out of ink
And ways to say (with a wink),
"I love you."

A Poem to the World

An old man, sitting on the shore,
Gazing past the ships at sea,
Pondering what might have been
Wishing how the world should be.

His body bears the scars received
From two wars that he believed
Would change the world and make it safe;
But now he feels he was deceived.

And why was he the one so spared,
Blessed with children and a wife,
While others never had a prayer
To carry out their dreams in life?

Brave men, no doubt, patriots too,
Dressed in brown and gray and blue,
Sent to kill year after year
For reasons not exactly clear.

And those who died from senseless crimes
During this, the best of times,
Passion, anger, greed and grime,
Victims cut short in their prime,

Now as he gazes from the shore,
He imagines he can see
An isle, far on the horizon,
People striving to be free

Of meanness and hostility
Hatred, animosity,
People coming to this isle
To talk together for a while.

People from all breeds and clans,
Faiths and nations and domains,
It must stop here, it must stop now,
Is their common new refrain.

With one accord they do proclaim,
No more carnage, wasted might,
Sending children out to fight,
While mothers cry into the night.

So on this isle of sanity,
Far from war's profanity,
They offer words of hope and cheer,
Kindness and humanity.

They say the generation next
Has to find a way to cope,
Forgive, not hate, must be the text,
Reason, mercy, joy and hope.

The old man, sitting on the shore,
Gazes past the ships at sea,
Prays that here forevermore
An old man's vision comes to be.

Time to Waste

A few spare moments
with nothing to do
and no place to be
and no one talking
no music playing
nowhere to rush to
just sit and reflect
on the gentle gift
of a little time
preciously wasted.

Inspirational Snapshots

Political Rancor
How did we become
so determined
to make enemies
out of each other?

First Peek
At the first peek
of daylight
I give thanks
for another day.

This Day
Be still
and know
that life
is gift.

A Walk in the Park
A walk in the park
a vigorous stroll,
it's good for the heart
and great for the soul.

Lasting Gift
Smiles of loved ones
linger in the memory
after everything else
has faded away.

Good Morning
In the quiet coolness
of the early morning
the soul is recharged.

Summer Beaches
Long walks on beaches
are better for my soul
than motivational
speeches.

What's Important
We always manage
to find time for
what's important.
Or do we?

Thank You
Your smile
brightened my day
and I should have
stopped to say thank you.

A New Day
Were these flowers
that colorful yesterday –
or was I just not
paying attention?

My Friend
My friend
knows me
inside and out,
and likes me
anyway.

Went for a Walk Instead
God, I apologize
for not going
to church today;
you shouldn't
have made this day
quite so gorgeous.

Overflowing
My cup overflows
with beauty
I cannot describe
and grace
I do not deserve.

Bravo!

Bravo I say,
bravo to you
for giving it
your very best.
Bravo, bravo!

At Seventeen

I wish I had known then
what I realize now
I didn't know then.

Quiet Time

On this end of the pond
swims one lonely duck –
maybe not lonely at all,
just needing a break
from all the other ducks
and their constant
quacking.

The Treatment Is Better than the Cure

Every month he goes for treatment
to another city three hundred miles away.
He has learned to cherish the drive time
as he cherishes every day now as a gift.

In the fall, he especially notices
the changing colors and temperatures.
In the winter, even the barren landscape
looks beautiful, given his state of mind.

Spring has to be his favorite season -
new life, new beauty, new possibilities.
Summer warmth soothes his weary bones
and reminds him of carefree days of his youth.

Usually he sticks to the interstate highway,
the quickest course from here to there.
But sometimes he chooses the back roads
through the small towns of simpler times.

Along the way he reflects on his own life,
on paths taken, not always for the best.
He has regrets, but not all that many,
and quietly he says a prayer for forgiveness.

Most of his prayers, though, reflect his joy
for grace extended along the journey.
These days his life seems focused on grace,
knowing that is how it always should be.

Morning Songs

Before the day gets too busy
I take a few minutes to be still and quiet
and listen to the birds singing their songs,
and they remind me that whatever I do today
will not make any difference to them.

I Have Been Diagnosed
with a Fatal Disease

I have been diagnosed with a fatal disease.
Everyone who gets this disease eventually dies.

I don't know how long I have, but I think
I should try to make the most of every day.

Come to terms with what is ultimately important.
Spend more time with those I love.

Take more time to appreciate every breath,
every sunrise, every kiss, every smile, every word.

Worry less and enjoy more.
Make my corner of the world a little better place.

For, after all, I don't know how much longer
I will be around.

I have been diagnosed with a fatal disease.
It's called life – and there is no cure.

Lord, We Thank You for Your Blessings

Tune: Hymn to Joy

Lord we thank you for your blessings,
for the blessings of this day,
Undeserving of your goodness,
we are grateful as we pray,
Keep us close to you for guidance,
free our hearts from greed and sin,
May we know you as our savior,
as our teacher, as our friend.

Come we here in adoration,
voices joined to sing your praise,
In this hour recharge our spirit,
fill us with your love and grace,
Give us wisdom, give us vision,
give us purpose is our prayer,
Let us serve you out of gladness,
out of joy we choose to share.

Make our lives a good example,
living temples of your word,
Smiles and tears we have for service,
gifts we offer to you, Lord,
Send us forth to live the Gospel,
spreading kindness far and near,
Love and mercy, peace and justice,
to a world that longs to hear.

Two Old Men Eating Chinese Food

I wrote this poem after having lunch with my writer friend, Carlton Stowers. Carlton and I would later team up to produce a book, 101 Essential Texas Books.

To the other diners in the restaurant,
they look like two old men eating Chinese food.

Who would know that both of them have written books
that sold quite a few copies at their peak

that both of them have endured personal crises
that dramatically changed their perspectives on life

that both have been divorced twice and watched
the infirmities of old age ravage their loved ones

that both have traveled separate roads that now
seem more like parallel paths at this stage of their lives

that both still think of themselves as ages they used to be
in spite of what the bathroom mirror may reveal.

To the other diners in the restaurant, they look like
what they are – two old men eating Chinese food.

Golf Haiku

The traditional Japanese haiku poem has just 17 syllables — 5 in the first line, 7 in the second, 5 in the third, about like the average golfer's score on the first three holes.

Four hours with friends
cursing a little white ball:
a good round of golf.

Can't find ball out here —
pretty bad slice, I admit —
middle of freeway!

Riding in a cart,
cool refreshment between holes —
it sure beats walking.

A dozen golf balls
lost in rough or hit in lake —
only the eighth hole.

On buying golf balls:
two boxes personalized —
they stay in the bag.

Another ball lost –
only penalty assessed:
the price of the ball.

An outstanding course:
great view, terrific pro shop,
well-stocked nineteenth hole.

Idyllic golf course:
picturesque setting, lush greens,
and name your own par.

Break after nine holes,
three cool ones in the clubhouse –
ready for back nine.

Just stay in clubhouse,
have two or three more scotches –
won't matter who wins.

A lucky shot indeed:
nine iron lands three feet from cup –
and so does the ball.

Frustrated by game,
he tosses club ninety yards –
he should throw, not hit!

That majestic oak
has survived despite attacks
from psycho golfers.

A perfect straight drive:
two hundred yards and counting –
only in my dreams.

Need to be prepared –
weekend trip to the in-laws,
golf clubs in the trunk.

Too much time on course,
too little time with wife and kids –
they could be caddies!

A great day for golf –
no clouds in the sky, which means
surely it will rain!

Three scramble partners
roll their eyes on the first shot:
he won't be much help.

Shook hands on golf course
after consummating deal;
they can write it off.

Seven-iron trusted
to get ball up over tree;
didn't quite work out.

Go to driving range –
hit straight two-hundred-yard drives
when it doesn't count.

First, address the ball:
You blankety-blank-blank ball!
Knock hell out of it.

He made a tough par
and everybody ducked
when he shouted "Four!"

Golf ball a teaser –
small, round, dimpled, inviting –
with mind of its own.

Expensive golf shirt,
new wide-brimmed classy straw hat,
same lousy golf game.

Built big home on course;
they sit, alert, in back yard,
count golf balls in pool.

I could shoot eighty
if I played every day –
and fudged a little.

He improved his lie:
used to claim he shot ninety –
now says eighty-five.

Golf is a great game
for teaching humility;
yeah, but who needs that?

Shot a hole-in-one,
got his name in the paper,
never played again.

Preacher doesn't swear;
has designated curser
as golfing partner.

Score doesn't matter;
the joy of being outside,
banging head on tree.

Don't Give Me a Fruitcake
for Christmas

Don't give me a fruitcake for Christmas this fall.
The last one you gave me I couldn't eat at all.

What are those green things and blue things and red?
Are they still alive, or dormant, or dead?

I knew I couldn't eat it, right from the start,
because of my liver - or kidney, or heart.

I didn't want to be seen as a jerk,
so I just boxed it up and took it to work.

No one would touch it and by the end of the day,
not even the ants would take it away.

I offered slices to my former best friends.
They haven't spoken a word to me since.

I fed it to the dogs and they turned up their noses
and busted the fence and trampled the roses.

I put it outside when they made such a fuss,
and I wasn't surprised when it started to rust.

I tried it as a prop to hold open the door.
It left a gooey spot on the hallway floor.

I put it on the end of a ten-foot pole,
and dropped it to the bottom of a ten-foot hole...

And poured in gasoline and threw in a torch.
But the next day there it was, right back on my porch.

I finally gave it to my Aunt Ida Mary.
(You probably noticed her obituary.)

We buried it with her... and three days later –
it showed up again in my refrigerator.

And there it has stayed for the rest of the year,
gobbling my pickles and guzzling my beer...

Inhaling the whipped cream and butterscotch custard,
the blackberry jelly and a new jar of mustard.

I'm stuck with it now, for worse, not for better.
That's why I'm transcribing this urgent letter.

I beg you: Don't give me a fruitcake this season.
I'll refuse to accept it. I don't need a reason.

The Plumber's Night Before Christmas

'Tis the night before Christmas, the plumber's here late,
trying to unclog our toilet, at double overtime rate.

The problems all started, as best we can tell,
when Aunt Nora went to the potty and stayed for a spell.

We knocked on the door, several times in fact,
but Nora wouldn't be disturbed, and that was that.

Then what to our innocent ears should explode
but the cries of Aunt Nora, still on the commode.

"Hey, something," she said, "is seriously wrong,
the water keeps rising, and it won't be too long......

"Until the pot overflows and we have quite a mess.
We must call the plumber," she had to confess.

So I called the plumber, the one we call Gator,
he said he could come, not sooner, but later.

He arrived in six hours, not in his Chevrolet,
but with eight reindeer pulling a really cool sleigh.

Instead of the carport, they landed on the roof,
and he hollered instructions to the reindeer on hoof.

"Whoa, Bucket and Reamer, stay, Faucet and Sink,
and Number One and Plunger, and Number Two and Stink.

Gator didn't have on his old jeans that night;
he was dressed all in red, trimmed crisply in white.

No butt cracks were showing as he bent down to work,
and took out his flashlight to look into the murk.

We were holding our breath when he went to his truck,
then he came back and offered a prayer of good luck.

He scratched his white head, then broke out in a smile.
"It's not a big problem," he said after a while.

"You have a small stoppage and that we can fix.
Apparently someone has flushed their toothpicks."

He reached in his pocket and pulled out a chain,
then began to stuff it down the clogged drain.

Before long we heard a rumble and a roar;
the potty was flowing, it was stopped up no more.

Then what to our wondering eyes should appear
but Santa in our fridge pulling out a cold beer.

He took a long swig, said, "Thanks for the brew;
it's Christmas Eve folks, I'm not charging you."

He hitched up the reindeer; we were all in a hush.
"Merry Christmas," he called, "and to all a good flush!

And Other Musings

If you've ever wished you could be king for just a little while, maybe you can relate to the opening piece in this concluding section - "Who Died and Made You King?" I wouldn't really want to be king for very long, just long enough for a few pertinent (or impertinent) pronouncements.

"Inlaws and Outlaws" and "My Dog, Your Dog" poke a little fun at our biases and prejudices. Other reflections in this section concern beer, fishing, baseball, working, giving thanks, and recognizing the every-day powers that we have, and I close with a short benediction.

Thanks for letting me share some serious and not-so-serious musings in these pages. I hope that, along the way, a few of them may have warmed your soul and brightened your spirit.

Who Died and Made You King?

Last time I checked, no one had died and made me king. But if they did, I would change things (for the better, I humbly submit) with a few pertinent decrees to address life's little annoyances and distractions - and maybe some concerns a tad more serious as well.

Herewith, forthwith, therewith, and upwith these decrees:

- No subject shall be permitted to present a complaint - in person or in writing or over the phone - until he or she has first offered two compliments.

- All businesses and agencies shall provide a live (and cheerful) human being to answer the telephone during business hours. Automated answering systems shall only be activated at nights and on weekends.

- Television crews broadcasting college football games are herewith required to also televise the halftime marching band performances in full.

- i shall come before e even after c.

- Graduation speeches shall be limited to ten minutes, max.

- All church services shall include at least five hymns known by, and in the vocal range of, the majority of the members.

- The price of roses shall be regulated during the first two weeks of February.

- All parents shall read to their children at least three times a week commencing at any time before a child's first birthday and continuing until the child reaches the age of nine.

- Throwing chewing gum on the ground shall be a felony offense.

- Every fast-food chain shall designate someone as Vice President for Clean Restrooms, paid at the executive level and held accountable.

- Instead of overtime periods to break ties in college football or basketball games, coaches shall choose eleven players from each team in football (five in basketball) to meet at the center of the field for an academic shoot-out of questions concerning science, math, history, geography, and literature.

- Small family fishing ponds shall be built in cities and liberally stocked with perch. Parents may help their children bait hooks, but only children shall be allowed to actually catch any fish.

- "Right to Complain" cards shall be distributed at voting places. People who do not vote shall have no "Right to Complain."

- Only people weighing less than a hundred and twenty pounds shall be sold a middle seat in an airline coach section.

- All presidents, chief executive officers, and chairmen of the board are herewith ordered to spend one day a year doing an entry-level job at their company – at entry-level pay. Yes, even the king.

- Movie theaters shall include a free bag of popcorn with every ticket.

- Ice skating shall henceforth be classified an art, like ballet, not a sport.

- Any location selling gasoline shall provide, at no charge, air and water hoses that work.

- Televised political commercials are herewith eliminated for being hazardous to our civic health.

- A flock of pigeons shall be specially trained to seek out and decorate cars taking up two parking spaces.

- The word "sucks" shall no longer be used as a synonym for "is bad."

- All uneaten fruitcakes may be turned in at the Fruitcake Recycling Center, where they shall be crushed and used to fill potholes.

- All committee meetings are herewith limited to one hour.

- Parents at children's sporting events are not allowed to speak. They may applaud.

Inlaws & Outlaws

Our family never goes to bed hungry.
Their family never goes to bed sober.

Our family lives high on the hog.
Their family lives like pigs.

Our family came across with the Pilgrims.
Their family comes across as turkeys.

Our family traces its roots to King James.
Their family traces its roots to Jim Beam.

Our family wrestles to pay its bills on time.
Their family arm-wrestles to see who pays the tab at closing time.

Our family has its faults.
Their family celebrates its faults.

Our family knows geography.
Their family knows it's 5 o'clock somewhere.

Our family puts together jigsaw puzzles on family night.
Their family picks up the pieces after family fights.

Our family takes Communion.
Their family guzzles wine.

Our family has lawn furniture.
Their family has furniture on the lawn.

Our family parks its cars in the garage.
Their family parks its cars in the front yard.

Our family has a couch in the front room.
Their family has a couch on the front porch.

Our family says grace before meals.
Their family says rub-a-dub-dub thanks for the grub.

Our family goes to outdoor concerts.
Their family goes to outdoor toilets.

Our family is well meaning.
Their family is, well, mean.

Our family lists the homeless mission as one of its
    favorite charities.
Their family lists the homeless mission as one of its
    favorite restaurants.

Our family brushes its teeth.
Their family doesn't have many teeth.

Our family pulls over for ambulances.
Their family chases ambulances.

Our family eats sushi.
Their family eats the bait.

Our family is paying off its mortgage.
Their family is paying off its bail bonds.

Our family has one or two weird relatives.
Their family has one or two normal ones.

Our family named its pet armadillo Tex.
Their family named its pet armadillo Dinner.

Our family speaks in complete sentences.
Their family completes jail sentences.

Our family goes on sabbatical.
Their family goes AWOL.

Our family is featured in Who's Who in America.
Their family is featured on America's Most Wanted.

Our family writes poetry to each other.
Their family writes rhymes on bathroom stalls.

Our family invests in the stock market.
Their family invests in lottery tickets.

Our family makes homemade ice cream.
Their family makes home brew.

Our family gets summoned for jury duty.
Their family gets summoned for trial.

Our family loves sunshine.
Their family loves moonshine.

Our family congratulates the cook after dinner.
Their family belches.

Our family passes out compliments.
Their family passes out.

Our family isn't perfect.
Their family isn't sane.

My Dog, Your Dog

When my dog barks, it is simply expressing itself. When your dog barks, it is being obnoxious.

Same holds for our opinions. Mine are based on deeply held convictions. Yours are radical.

My outrageous idea is an example of "thinking outside the box." Yours is weird.

I just want to get things done. You are compulsive.

I am running a little late. You are never on time.

My child is intelligent. Your child is a smart-aleck.

My youngster is full of life. Yours is wild.

The students at my school have a feisty spirit. The students at your school are bad sports.

My team plays hard. Your team plays rough.

My religion is true. Yours is fanatical.

And so it goes. It depends on our perspective in how we view our dogs, as well as our families, our faith, our politics, our outlook on life.

My dog could use a bath.
Your dog is filthy.

My dog is a good watchdog.
Your dog barks all the time.

My dog is a mixed breed.
Your dog is a mutt.

My dog stories are interesting.
Your dog stories are tedious.

My dog is provoked only when threatened.
Your dog is vicious.

My dog drools a little.
Your dog slobbers.

My dog sings.
Your dog wails.

My dog is saving its energy.
Your dog is lazy.

My dog greets the mail carrier.
Your dog snarls at the postman.

My dog loves people.
Your dog jumps on people.

My dog has to go when nature calls.
Your dog makes a mess in everyone's yard.

My dog likes to kiss.
Your dog sticks its tongue in people's faces.

My dog smiles.
Your dog bares its teeth.

My dog takes time to smell the flowers.
Your dog digs up the flowers.

My dog can't help it that it sheds a little fur.
Your dog gets hair all over everything in the house.

My dog needs a tooth-brushing.
Your dog has disgusting breath.

My dog jumps for joy.
Your dog jumps for cookies.

My dog loves firemen.
Your dog loves fire hydrants.

My dog accepts me unconditionally.
Your dog accepts you anyway.

A Beer for My Brother

As the story goes, a man walks into a bar and orders two mugs of beer.

"One at a time?" the bartender asks.

"No, both at the same time. You see, I have a brother who doesn't live here anymore. When he moved away, we agreed that we would remember the days when we could have a beer together. So I'm drinking one for my brother and one for myself."

The bartender says that's a nice gesture and sets two mugs of beer in front of him. He takes a sip from one, then from the other until both are empty. Then he orders a second round for both of them.

The man becomes a regular, always ordering – and drinking - two mugs every time, then a second round.

One day he comes in and orders just one mug and drains it. Orders another. Drains it.

The regulars in the bar get very quiet.

The bartender says, "I don't mean to intrude on your grief, but I'm sorry about your brother."

The man seems puzzled at first. Then he smiles.

"Oh, no one has died," he says. "It's just that my wife and I joined the Baptist church, and I had to quit drinking…

"Hasn't stopped my brother, though."

Hope, Faith, and Fishing

On one of my first fishing trips as a boy, my dad asked if I was having fun fishing.

"It's not the fishing I like," I am reported to have replied, "it's the catching."

However, as I have gotten older, I have come to appreciate that, often, the process can be more satisfying than the results.

That is one of the lessons that fishing teaches us. There are many others.

I believe we can find deeper meaning in almost any activity if we try hard enough. In fishing, one doesn't have to try all that hard, actually, to find lessons of significance that apply to all of life.

Once when I was fishing, I kept getting my line caught in an overhead tree, which prompted my partner to remind me, "You're not going to catch many fish in a tree."

The same goes for business or any other enterprise – you've got to go where the fish are if you hope to be successful.

You've heard it said that the two happiest days in a man's life are the day he buys his first boat – and the day he sells it. Isn't that how it is in other facets of life?

We think that our life will be complete/perfect if we can just acquire such-and-such. Eventually we learn – or should - that satisfaction doesn't come from things, but from within ourselves.

Fishing has entered our language in ways that don't have anything to do with fish.

We *fish* for compliments. We *fish* around for information. We *bait* an opponent in a debate. We *lure* someone into an argument.

We *toss out a line* in a speech. We are told to *fish or cut bait* when we need to make a commitment. We *bite* or fall for things *hook, line and sinker.*

I've never been convinced that it was important to be quiet when you're fishing. Do we think the fish are listening to our conversations?

It's probably just a ploy by fishermen to gain themselves a little peace and quiet, which isn't a bad idea at that.

Fishing gets your mind off your troubles. Your focus is on catching fish, and everything else is put on hold for a while.

When you do return to reality, often you do so with a clearer perspective.

A cane pole and a can of worms is the low-tech version of fishing, sort of like writing on a manual typewriter or with pad and pencil.

You don't *have* to have a lot of expensive equipment to get the job done.

Although a lot of fishing takes place on lakes and rivers on Sunday morning, fishing has religious significance in the Christian community.

Jesus picked fishermen as disciples and used fishing analogies to illustrate points.

The fish was an early Christian symbol and has enjoyed renewed popularity in recent years.

The little boy in the parable of feeding the five thousand had five loaves and two fishes, not two boxes of fried chicken. In the modern version, he would have five hush puppies and two catfish fillets.

If fishing teaches any virtue especially well, it teaches patience. The fisherman can't do anything to force the fish to bite. He can only keep tossing the bait out there and wait for some action.

Patience, as most fishermen know, is an overrated virtue.

Fishing also teaches about hope and faith – *hoping* that the next time you toss out your line will be the one when the fish grabs it, and then actually *believing* that will happen.

Fishing probably does not teach another virtue very well – telling the truth. The fish get bigger and more abundant the more their stories are told.

The one that got away always seems to get exaggerated as the years pass – and not just in fishing. The opportunity that got away; the championship game that was lost; the idea that somebody else developed; the job that somebody else was in the right place for, at the right time.

The best rule is not to dwell on the ones that got away but make the most of the ones that didn't.

Baseball and Windshield Wipers

Baseball, hot dogs, apple pie, and… windshield wipers.

Windshield wipers?

The story goes way back sixty or more years ago. I was still in high school and coached a Little League team – the Yankees – for several summers.

This particular summer we had an especially enthusiastic group of 11- and 12-year-old boys on the team. Some groups – some teams – you just enjoy more than others. This was one of those special teams.

As a high school senior with almost constant access to the family car, it fell my duty to be the chauffeur. We put a lot of miles on the '57 Ford that summer shuttling between our little town and the ballpark seven miles away.

The windshield washer on our '57 Ford was controlled by a small pedal on the floorboard. When the pedal was depressed, the washer would squirt water on the windshield, and the wipers would wipe one time, then cut off.

However, on one of our trips from the ballpark, I depressed the pedal to squirt water to clean off the windshield and discovered the washer was empty. But the windshield wipers still wiped once, then turned off.

"You boys want to see my voice-activated windshield wiper?" I asked. "Look, I can just say *windshield wiper* and the windshield wiper will come on."

They were skeptical.

"Windshield wiper," I commanded. The windshield wiper wiped once, then stopped.

"How did you do that?" asked Roy, whom we had nicknamed Duck.

"I guess it's magic," I said. "It just responds to voice commands." I did it again. "Windshield wiper." It wiped once, then stopped.

Ricky thought he had it figured out. "He's pushing a button on the steering wheel." I took both hands off the steering wheel. "Windshield wiper." Wipe. Stop.

"Let me try it," Duck said. "Windshield wiper." Nothing.

"Windshield wiper," Ricky said. Wipe. Stop.

"I guess it doesn't recognize your voice, Duck," I said. "It worked for Ricky."

Sometimes it's not very hard to entertain 11- and 12-year-old boys. This was one of those times. I milked the windshield wiper trick the rest of the Little League season before one of the boys finally figured it out.

There is no moral, no philosophical or political significance to this tale. Just a baseball story that comes to mind on a hot, lazy summer day, when grown men sometimes remember when they weren't.

Any Kind of a Hit Will Do

To the Little Leaguer
playing second base
and now at the plate,
two on and two out,
score tied, sixth inning,
everything rides
on this one pitch.
He will find out in time
that it really doesn't,
but right now it really does.

Work, Work, Work, Work

We love to work.

We hate to work.

We work to put money in our pockets.

We work to put meaning in our lives.

We work to support our families.

We work to support our egos.

We work at home.

We work to get away from home.

We work hard.

We work harder.

We work hardest.

We work hardly.

We work to get ahead.

We work to get by.

We work to stay put.

We work to move on.

We work to accomplish something.

We work to get credit.

We work to make a difference.

We work to eat.

We work to learn.

We work to be with people.

We work in spite of people.

We work out.

We work around.

We work until.

We work for.

We work toward.

We work on.

We work up.

We work to be satisfied.

We work to satisfy someone else.

We work to succeed.

We work to hang on.

We work to earn a living.

We work to get on with living.

We work to earn a rest.

We work while we're resting.

We work too much.

We work too long.

We work too little.

We work for fun.

We work to pay the bills.

We work to be respectable.

We work to be responsible.

We work to be rewarded.

We work together.

We work in teams.

We work alone.

We work for them.

We work for us.

We work because we have to.
We work because we want to.
We work because we ought to.
We work because we need to.
We work just because.

Giving Thanks for the Simple Things

We have two preachers on my wife's side of the family, and another rather reverent cousin. So when we would get together for extended family celebrations, one of them was usually expected/honored to offer thanks before we sat down to eat.

But they weren't there for the everyday meals, and as the resident preacher's son/church elder/oldest male, it often fell my lot to say grace, especially if we were having dinner with my mother-in-law.

The preachers/reverent cousin are much more expressive than I am. I don't know how they summon so much divine eloquence, but I suppose it is because they have a closer relationship with the Provider than I do. Or maybe they've just done a lot more praying, in all situations.

Anyway, when it was pretty obvious that everyone expected me to say grace, I kept it pretty simple.

If we'd had a little rain, I might say, "Thank you, God, for the rain and for this food. Amen."

If we were having take-out pizza, my prayer might be simply, "Thank you, God, for pizza."

Usually, I would pitch in a thank you for the "many blessings" and for the "beautiful day" and for the "good food," especially when it came to recognizing my mother-in-law's and my wife's contributions.

But if we were having leftovers (and I love leftovers), I might just pray – and mean it - "Thank you, God, for leftovers!" And we would all smile and sit down to eat.

The point is that we should be grateful every day for the "many blessings" that we too often take for granted. And for the food, even takeout pizza and leftovers.

If it's more than that, maybe there's a preacher or reverent cousin available to handle it.

We Have the Power

We don't have control over a lot of things in our lives. But it's easy to let that be an excuse for not using all the power we do have.

We have the power to smile.

We have the power to be kind.

We have the power to be courteous and pleasant.

We have the power to praise.

We have the power to offer a compliment.

We have the power to listen.

We have the power to encourage.

We have the power to make others feel important.

We have the power to try.

We have the power to care.

We have the power to do our best.

We have the power to be truthful and honest.

We have the power to participate.

We have the power to give.

We have the power to vote.

We have the power to be optimistic.

We have the power to be happy.

We have the power to treat others with respect.

We have the power to make a difference.

We do not lack for power. We just need to recognize what we have and make the best use of it.

A Blessing

May your days be filled with beauty,
your hours with joy,
your moments with peace,
and your life with grace.

Acknowledgments

Special thanks to family members and friends who read the manuscript, offered encouragement, made helpful suggestions, and caught mistakes – Carol Dromgoole, Jennifer LeBow, Charlie Dromgoole, Carlton Stowers, Jay Moore, Loretta Fulton, Diane Kelly, and Joe Specht.

Section 1: "Civility Champions" is adapted from a similar essay in *More Civility, Please,* Texas Star Trading, 2016, out of print.

You may have read a few of the lines from "They're Singing Our Song" in church newsletters or the internet, but not in as much "depth" as I have plunged.

I included a similar version of "A Long-Stemmed Rose" in *The Power of a Penny,* St. Martin's Press, 1999.

"Try Giving Yourself Away" and "Teachers Two by Two" appeared in *Book Guy,* Texas Star Trading, 2018.

"What Grandchildren Do" was first published as a picture book - *What Grandchildren Do,* Willow Creek Press, 2007, out of print.

Section 2: "Thanks for Showing Up" is similar to a piece in *The Power of a Penny.*

"In the Spirit" was in *A Little Cup of Kindness*, Bright Sky Press, 2007, out of print.

"A Sermon About Patience" previously ran as "A Prayer for Patience" in *A Little Cup of Kindness.*

I am not the original source for "The Agnostic's Sermon," and I have no idea where it came from. It's something I've heard all my adult life.

"Stable Gifts for Today" appeared in *West Texas Christmas Stories,* Abilene Christian University Press, 2013.

Section 3: "Any Semicolons Around Here?" ran in *West Texas Stories,* ACU Press, 2016.

"Aha!" was in *I've Been Diagnosed with a Fatal Disease and other poems,* Texas Star Trading, 2008, out of print.

Section 4: "Middle Names" and "Vote Dry!" are from *A Small Town in Texas,* State House Press, 2004, out of print.

The poems I quote by David Davis are from his book, *Texas Mother Goose,* Pelican, 2006.

"The Cowboy Spirit: Lessons for Life" is taken from my book, *Cowboys at Heart,* Sourcebooks, 2005, out of print.

Section 5: As noted in the introduction to this section, four of the stories previously appeared in *Coleman Springs USA,* ACU Press, 2012.

Section 6: Several of the poems in this section were included in my books, *A Little Cup of Kindness, I Have Been Diagnosed* *with a Fatal Disease and other poems,* and *More Civility, Please,* all out of print.

"Don't Give Me a Fruitcake for Christmas" appeared in prose format in *West Texas Christmas Stories.*

Section 7: "Hope, Faith, and Fishing" is adapted from my book, *I'd Rather Be Fishing,* Sourcebooks, 2005, out of print. That book was dedicated to my daughter, Janet, who died suddenly a few months after it was published.

I tweaked the story "A Beer for My Brother," based on a very similar story involving three brothers. I don't know the original source of that story.

"We Have the Power" ran in similar form in *The Power of a Penny.*

I included a version of "Baseball and Windshield Wipers" in *A Small Town in Texas* and the poem "Any Kind of a Hit Will Do" in *I Have Been Diagnosed with a Fatal Disease and other poems.*

About twenty of the pieces throughout the book were first composed as columns or guest columns for the *Abilene Reporter-News* and other publications.

About the Author

Glenn Dromgoole has written more than thirty books and edited and published dozens more. He was a newspaper writer and editor for thirty-five years before retiring to write, edit, publish, review, promote, and sell books. He and his wife Carol live in Abilene, Texas, where they operate Texas Star Trading Company, a book, gift, and gourmet shop.

He is a member of the Texas Literary Hall of Fame and the Texas A&M Journalism Hall of Honor, was named Abilene's Outstanding Citizen of the Year in 2013, and was presented the A.C. Greene Award for lifetime literary achievement in 2018. He co-chaired the West Texas Book Festival from 2001 to 2017 and wrote a weekly syndicated newspaper column on Texas Books from 2002 to 2020.

Books by Glenn Dromgoole

A Christmas Offering (1990)

A Trip to Russia (1991)

Stories (1992)

What Dogs Teach Us (1999)

I Like It When You Read to Me (1999)

The Perfect Hamburger (1999)

The Power of a Penny (1999)

What Cats Teach Us (2000)

What Puppies Teach Us (2001)

What Horses Teach Us (2002)

A Small Town in Texas (2004)

Learning from Longhorns, with Lester Galbreath (2004)

What Happy Dogs Know (2004)

I'd Rather Be Fishing (2005)

100 Great Things About Texas (2005)

Aggie Savvy (2005)

What Smart Cats Know (2005)

Cowboys at Heart (2005)

Good Night Cowboy (2006)

Good Night Cowgirl (2006)

A Little Cup of Kindness (2007)

What Grandchildren Do (2007)

I Have Been Diagnosed with a Fatal Disease (2008)

What Dogs Teach Us II (2008)

Parables from the Diamond, with Phil Christopher (2008)

Good Night Little Texan (2012)

Coleman Springs USA (2012)

Abilene Stories from Then to Now,
  with Jay Moore and Joe W. Specht (2013)

West Texas Christmas Stories (2013)

101 Essential Texas Books, with Carlton Stowers (2014)

Abilene A to Z, with Jay Moore (2015)

West Texas Stories (2016)

More Civility, Please (2016)

Book Guy (2018)

Just Happy to Be Here (2022)